# Teaching
## in a
# Special Education
# Classroom

*This book is dedicated to my wife, Jackie, and my two children, Jacqueline and Scott, who provide me with the love and purpose for undertaking projects that I hope will enhance the lives of others. My life has been blessed by their loving presence.*

*I also dedicate this book to my parents, who provided me with the secure and loving foundation from which to grow; my sister, Carol, who makes me smile and laugh; and my brother-in-law, George, who has always been a positive guiding light in my professional journey.*

—R. P.


*This book is dedicated to my wife, Anita, and two children, Collin and Brittany, who give me the greatest life imaginable. The long hours and many years it took to finish this book would never have been possible without the support of my loving wife. Her constant encouragement, understanding, and love provide me with the strength I need to accomplish my goals. I thank her with all my heart. I also dedicate this book to my parents, who have given me support and guidance throughout my life. Their words of encouragement and guidance have made my professional journey a rewarding and successful experience.*

—G. G.

A STEP-BY-STEP GUIDE FOR EDUCATORS

# Teaching
## in a
# Special Education
# Classroom

ROGER PIERANGELO ~ GEORGE GIULIANI

Skyhorse Publishing, Inc.

Skyhorse Publishing books may be purchased in bulk at special discounts for sales
promotion, corporate gifts, fund-raising, or educational purposes. Special
editions can also be created to specifications. For details, contact the Special
Sales Department, Sky Pony Press, 307 West 36th Street, 11th Floor,
New York, NY 10018 or info@skyhorsepublishing.com.

Skyhorse® and Skyhorse Publishing® are registered trademark of Skyhorse Publishing,
Inc.®, a Delaware corporation.

Visit our website at www.skyhorsepublishing.com.

10 9 8 7 6 5 4 3 2 1

Library of Congress Cataloging-in-Publication Data is available on file.

Cover design by Michael Dubowe

Print ISBN: 978-1-63450-718-9
Ebook ISBN: 978-1-63450-719-6

Printed in the United States of America

# Contents

Preface                                                                    xi

Acknowledgments                                                            xiii

About the Authors                                                          xv

Step I.    What to Do Before the School Term Begins:
           Getting to Know Your Students                                    1

Step II.   Designing and Setting Up Your Classroom                         11
           Part I: Designing the Special Education Classroom                11
               Station-Oriented Model                                       11
               Child-Oriented Model                                         13
               Teacher-Oriented Model                                       13
           Part II: Setting Up Your Inclusion Classroom                     13
               Helpful Sites for Information on Setting Up
                   a Classroom                                              16
           Part III: Evaluating Existing Materials                          16

Step III.  Meeting With Parents and Staff Members                          19
           Part I: Communicating With Parents                              19
               Learn How to Conduct Effective Parent
                   Conferences                                              19
               Communicating With Parents for Primary
                   Inclusion Teachers                                       22
               Communicating With Parents for Secondary
                   Inclusion Teachers                                       24
           Part II: Meeting With Your Assistant Teacher or
               Aide Before School Begins (Special
               Education Class)                                             25
               Meet With Your Inclusion Team Teacher
                   (Inclusion Class)                                        27
           Part III: Communicating With Related-Service
               Providers (All Settings)                                    29

Part IV: Communicating With Your Student's
Regular Education Teachers (Resource
Room Teachers)                                          30
Part V: Communicating With the Mainstreaming
Team and Classroom Teachers (Self-Contained
Class)                                                 32

Step IV.   **Factors Affecting Curriculum**
           **Performance for Students With Special Needs**    **35**
           Factors Affecting Curriculum                   36
               Academic Factors                           36
               Environmental Factors                      37
               Intellectual Factors                       38
               Language Factors                           38
               Medical Factors                            39
               Perceptual Factors                         40
               Psychological Factors                      40
               Social Factors                             42

Step V.    **Adapting the Curriculum for**
           **Students With Special Needs**                    **43**
           What Are Curriculum Adaptations?                43
               Examples of Curriculum Adaptation          44
               Assessing Student Progress                 45
           Ways to Adapt the Curriculum                    46
               Strategies for Adapting Tests and Quizzes  49
           Adapting Response Mode                          51

Step VI.   **Classroom Management of**
           **Children With Specific Disabilities**            **53**
           Students With Learning Disabilities             54
               Adjust the Means of Presentation and
                   Evaluation                              54
           Students With Mental Retardation                56
               Techniques for Teaching Children
                   With Mental Retardation                56
               Vocational and Career Skill Development     58
           Students With Emotional Disabilities            59
               Helping the Student Complete Classwork
                   Assignments                            59
           Students With Attention Deficit/Hyperactivity
           Disorder                                        59
               Organization                               59
               Academic Skills                            60

Step VII.  **Apply Instructional Interventions for Specific Behaviors Exhibited in the Classroom by Students With Emotional and/or Behavioral Disorders**                    61

Instructional Interventions for Active
  Noncompliance                                                    61
    Examples of Behavior                                           61
    Desired Alternative Behavior(s)                                62
    General Instructional Strategies That Might
      Be Useful in Teaching the Desired
      Behavior(s)                                                  62
Instructional Interventions for Attendance
  Problems                                                         63
    Examples of Behavior                                           63
    Desired Alternative Behavior(s)                                63
    General Instructional Strategies That Might
      Be Useful in Teaching the Desired
      Behavior(s)                                                  63
Instructional Interventions for Difficulty With
  Transitions                                                      65
    Examples of Behavior                                           65
    Desired Alternative Behavior(s)                                65
    General Instructional Strategies That Might
      Be Useful in Teaching the Desired
      Behavior(s)                                                  65
Instructional Interventions for Disrespect to
  Teachers                                                         66
    Examples of Behavior                                           66
    Desired Alternative Behavior(s)                                66
    General Instructional Strategies That Might
      Be Useful in Teaching the Desired
      Behavior(s)                                                  67
Instructional Interventions for Classroom
  Disruption                                                       67
    Examples of Behavior                                           67
    Desired Alternative Behavior(s)                                68
    General Instructional Strategies That Might
      Be Useful in Teaching the Desired
      Behavior(s)                                                  68
Instructional Interventions for Failure to Accept
  Responsibility for Own Behavior and/or
  Consequences for Misbehavior                                     69
    Examples of Behavior                                           69

Desired Alternative Behavior(s)      69

General Instructional Strategies That Might
Be Useful in Teaching the Desired
Behavior(s)      69

Instructional Interventions for Interpersonal
Relationships With Peers      70

Examples of Behavior      70

Desired Alternative Behavior(s)      70

General Instructional Strategies That Might
Be Useful in Teaching the Desired
Behavior(s)      70

Instructional Interventions for Out-of-Control
Behaviors      71

Examples of Behavior      71

Desired Alternative Behavior(s)      71

General Instructional Strategies That Might
Be Useful in Teaching the Desired
Behavior(s)      71

Instructional Interventions for Passive Resistance      71

Examples of Behavior      71

Desired Alternative Behavior(s)      72

General Instructional Strategies That Might
Be Useful in Teaching the Desired
Behavior(s)      72

Instructional Interventions for Not Respecting
Property or Personal Space of Others      73

Examples of Behavior      73

Desired Alternative Behavior(s)      73

General Instructional Strategies That Might
Be Useful in Teaching the Desired
Behavior(s)      73

Instructional Interventions for Verbal Aggression      74

Examples of Behavior      74

Desired Alternative Behavior(s)      74

General Instructional Strategies That Might
Be Useful in Teaching the Desired
Behavior(s)      74

Instructional Interventions for Verbal Outbursts      75

Examples of Behavior      75

Desired Alternative Behavior(s)      75

General Instructional Strategies That Might
Be Useful in Teaching the Desired
Behavior(s)      75

**Step VIII.**   **Understanding Grading Options**
**for Students With Special Needs**          77
    Grading Options                                  77
    Reporting to Parents                             79

**Step IX.**   **Developing Cooperative Educational**
**Plans for Your Students**                   85

**Step X.**   **End-of-School-Year Responsibilities**   89
    Triennial Evaluation Reports                     89
    Annual Review Meetings                           90
    Declassification Considerations and Procedures   92
    Extended School Year (ESY) Services              93
    End-of-School-Year Reports                       95
    Final Summary                                    96

**Glossary**                                        97

**References**                                      99

**Index**                                          101

# Preface

The *Step-by-Step Guide to Teaching in a Special Education Classroom* is aimed at providing educators with very practical advice on a variety of topics faced by special educators every day. The *Step-by-Step Guide to Teaching in a Special Education Classroom* will provide new teachers with practical guidelines for beginning the school year as a special education teacher and experienced teachers with supportive information that may help improve their classrooms.

You may be hired in the field of special education in a variety of settings, including a resource room, self-contained special class, or an inclusion setting. This book focuses on the various steps that should be taken to ensure the welfare of the children; the appropriate educational setting; information that should be gathered; communicating with related-service providers, parents, paraprofessionals, and assistant teachers; and other areas to make your job easier and more rewarding. This book assumes nothing and provides important information for all three settings. When noted, certain information is best suited for a specific type of setting. If not noted, then assume that the information being presented applies to all three settings.

This guide is formatted to provide a very practical, experience-based body of knowledge that assumes nothing and allows you to "hit the floor running" if you are placed in a job as a special education teacher on September 1.

# Acknowledgments

In the course of writing this book, we have encountered many professional and outstanding Web sites. Those resources have contributed and continue to contribute enormous information, support, guidance, and education to parents, students, and professionals in the area of special education. Although we have accessed many worthwhile sites, we especially thank and acknowledge the National Dissemination Center for Children with Disabilities, the U.S. Department of Education, and the National Institutes of Health.

Both Dr. Pierangelo and Dr. Giuliani extend sincere thanks to Allyson Sharpe, Laureen Shea, and Libby Larson for all of their hard work and dedication toward making this book a reality. We could not have completed it without your constant support and encouragement. We would also like to thank the following for their professional contributions to the book:

John Fry
Social Studies/Emotional Behavioral
   Disorder/Learning Disability Teacher
Care/Treatment and Special Education Department
Hopkins School District
Woodbury, MN

Teri Fechter
Special Education and Learning Disability Teacher
Franklin Elementary School
Little Chute, WI

Nicole Chiarello-Guyon
Special Education Teacher
Westerly School Department
Cranston, RI

**Roger Pierangelo:** I extend thanks to the following: the faculty, administration, and staff of the Department of Graduate Special Education and Literacy at Long Island University; Ollie Simmons, for her friendship, loyalty, and great personality; the students and parents of the Herricks Public Schools whom I have worked with and known over the past 35 years; the late Bill Smyth, a truly gifted and "extraordinary ordinary" man; and Helen Firestone, for her influence on my career and her tireless support.

**George Giuliani:** I extend sincere thanks to all of my colleagues at Hofstra University in the School of Education and Allied Human Services. I am especially grateful to those who have made my transition to Hofstra University such a smooth one, including Maureen Murphy (dean), Darra Pace (chairperson), Frank Bowe, Diane Schwartz (graduate program director of early childhood special education), Daniel Sciarra, Gloria Wilson, Laurie Johnson, Joan Bloomgarden, Jamie Mitus, Estelle Gellman, Holly Seirup, Adele Piombino, Marjorie Butler, and Eve Byrne. I also thank my brother and sister, Roger and Claudia; my mother-in-law, Ursula Jenkeleit; my sisters-in-law, Karen and Cindy; and my brothers-in-law, Robert and Bob. They have provided me with encouragement and reinforcement in all of my personal and professional endeavors.

# About the Authors

**Dr. Roger Pierangelo, PhD,** is an associate professor in the Department of Special Education and Literacy at Long Island University. He has been an administrator of special education programs; served for 18 years as a permanent member of Committees on Special Education; has over 30 years of experience in the public school system as a general education classroom teacher and school psychologist; and serves as a consultant to numerous private and public schools, PTA, and SEPTA groups. Dr. Pierangelo has also been an evaluator for the New York State Office of Vocational and Rehabilitative Services and a director of a private clinic. He is a New York State–licensed clinical psychologist, a certified school psychologist, and a Board Certified Diplomate Fellow in Student and Adolescent Psychology and Forensic Psychology. Dr. Pierangelo is the executive director of the National Association of Special Education Teachers (NASET) and an executive director of the American Academy of Special Education Professionals (AASEP). He also holds the office of vice president of the National Association of Parents with Children in Special Education (NAPCSE).

Dr. Pierangelo earned his BS from St. John's University, MS from Queens College, Professional Diploma from Queens College, PhD from Yeshiva University, and Diplomate Fellow in Student and Adolescent Psychology and Forensic Psychology from the International College of Professional Psychology. Dr. Pierangelo is a member of the American Psychological Association, New York State Psychological Association, Nassau County Psychological Association, New York State Union of Teachers, and Phi Delta Kappa.

Dr. Pierangelo is the coauthor of multiple books by Corwin Press, including *The Big Book of Special Education Resources* and the *Step-by-Step Guide for Educators* series.

**Dr. George Giuliani, JD, PsyD,** is a full-time tenured associate professor and the director of Special Education at Hofstra University's School of Education and Allied Human Services in the Department of Counseling, Research, Special Education, and Rehabilitation. Dr. Giuliani earned his BA from the College of the Holy Cross, MS from St. John's University, JD from City University Law School, and PsyD from Rutgers University, the Graduate School of Applied and Professional Psychology. He earned Board Certification as a Diplomate Fellow in Student and Adolescent Psychology and Forensic Psychology from the International College of Professional Psychology. Dr. Giuliani is also a New York State–licensed psychologist and certified school psychologist and has an extensive private practice focusing on students with special needs. He is a member of the American Psychological Association, New York State Psychological Association, National Association of School Psychologists, Suffolk County Psychological Association, Psi Chi, American Association of University Professors, and the Council for Exceptional Students.

Dr. Giuliani is the president of the National Association of Parents with Children in Special Education (NAPCSE), executive director of the National Association of Special Education Teachers (NASET), and executive director of the American Academy of Special Education Professionals (AASEP). He is a consultant for school districts and early childhood agencies and has provided numerous workshops for parents and guardians and teachers on a variety of special education and psychological topics. Dr. Giuliani is the coauthor of numerous books by Corwin Press, including *The Big Book of Special Education Resources* and the *Step-by-Step Guide for Educators* series.

# Step I

# What to Do Before the School Term Begins

## Getting to Know Your Students

The best advice in preparing for a new school year is to begin as early as possible. You can do many things before the start of school to facilitate your experience and make the school year more productive for you and your students. The first day of school should not be the first day you learn about your students. This would be a major mistake and inevitably make classroom management more difficult.

The very first step in setting up the room actually involves getting to know the students who will be in your classroom before the first day of school. It is imperative that you find out as much information about each student as possible so that you are fully prepared when the child walks into the room for the first time. You will be amazed at the wealth of materials available on each child if you know where to look. The only exception may be a student new to the school from another city or state for whom materials may not have yet arrived. If this is the case, there are several things you can still do, which we will discuss later. When working with students with disabilities, information on the child can be found in the following possible places:

- *History of educational enrollment:* Some of your students may have attended several different schools over the years. It will be important to determine the type of school (e.g., residential) to discover further information on the child's history. You should be able to deduce this information by the school names on the report cards found in the permanent folder. For some children with disabilities, this may be their first year in a mainstreamed school. They may require added attention and support in the transition.
- *Medical background:* A very important piece of information to gather will be the student's medical records. Many times, students with disabilities may have secondary health issues about which you will need to become informed. This information can be found in the school nurse's office. Pay close attention to vision and hearing levels, last eye and hearing examination (this should be within the last year), medications, allergies, and any other medical issues that might need attention in the classroom.
- *Primary record folder in main office:* Normally this piece of information is in the main office. While it should not contain any confidential information, such as psychological reports, it will contain a great deal of important information on the child's background. This folder should contain all the basic information on the child (e.g., phone, address, parents' names, date of birth, siblings' names and ages).
- *Prior comments from past teachers:* It will be very important for you to see how the child did in past years through the reports of past teachers. These items may be found in the permanent record folder or may be part of the child's report card forms. If they are not, you may need to interview the child's past teachers to gain some insight into strength and weakness patterns.
- *Report card history:* Report cards may show you patterns of performance in many academic areas, including both strengths and areas of concern. These should also be contained in the permanent record folder.
- *Group achievement scores:* This information can usually be found either pasted to the permanent record folder or inside the folder. These materials, if accurate, can also provide a pattern of strengths and areas in need of improvement. However, be very careful about drawing any conclusions from low scores unless other information backs up your impressions (e.g., classroom performance, teachers' reports). Sometimes children who are experiencing academic problems may not try as hard as possible for fear of failure. Consequently, the resulting scores may not reflect true achievement levels. You should also know the test

vocabulary and abbreviations used to report test information. Become familiar with the following:

o *Age Equivalent* (abbreviation would be *AE*): Some test scores will be presented in what are called Age Equivalents. This means that the score will be reflected in years and months (e.g., a score of 8–2 would represent an Age Equivalent score of 8 years and 2 months). Further, if your child is 7 years 8 months old and gets an Age Equivalent (AE) score of 8–2 (8 years 2 months) then your child is performing above age expectancy. If the AE score is 6–1 (6 years 1 month), then your child is performing below age expectancy.

o *Grade Equivalent* (abbreviation would be *GE*): Some test scores will be presented as Grade Equivalents. This means that the score will be reflected using grade level and months (e.g., 10–2 (10th grade 2nd month). You will want to compare this to your child's present grade level. Further, if your child's exact grade level is 5th grade 3rd month (5–3) and the Grade Equivalent (GE) score is 7–2 (7th grade 2nd month) then your child is performing above grade expectancy. If the score is 4–1 (4th grade 1st month), then the child is performing below grade expectancy.

o *Local Percentile/Local Percentile Rank* (abbreviation would be *LP* or *LPR*): This score compares your child's performance on a test against every other child of the same age within the school district. See *National Percentiles* for further explanation of the purposes of percentiles.

o *Mean* (abbreviation is *M*): The mean is the average. If someone says your child's "mean score" was 75, it means that when all the child's tests are added up, the average score, or mean, was 75. Suppose your child gets the following scores on a test: 75, 85, 90, 70. When you add these up (320) and divide by the number of tests (4), the average score, or mean, is 80.

o *National Percentile/National Percentile Rank* (abbreviation is *NP* or *NPR*): This score compares your child's performance on a test against that of every other child of the same age throughout the country. However, it is very important that you understand that *percentile* is not *percent*. The range for percentiles is 1–99 with the 99th percentile being the highest score possible. A percentile of 50 is right in the middle. For instance, if your child scores at the 65th percentile nationally, then that means that your child did better than approximately 65 percent of the children the same age and only 34 percent did better than your child. (Since percentile only goes up to 99, then 99 – 65 = 34.) If your child scores at the 23rd percentile nationally, then he or she did better than approximately 23 percent of the students the same age, and 76 percent did better (99 – 23 = 76).

In assessment, percentile ranks are very important because they indicate how well a child did when compared to the norms on a test. Knowing that a child had a percentile rank of 97 on a test would tell you that the child is exceptional in this testing area, while knowing that the percentile rank is 7 would tell you that this is an area of weakness.

o *Range:* If the teacher or psychologist says that the range of your child's scores was from 65–90, that represents your child's lowest score and highest score; all the other scores fell somewhere in between these two scores.

o *Raw Score* (abbreviation might be *RS*): This normally refers to the number of answers that your child answered correctly on any test. For instance, if your child answers 12 out of 20 questions correctly, then the Raw Score will be 12. In general, raw scores by themselves mean very little. For example, suppose a student in your class got 18 out of 20 correct on the spelling test. The number 18 has no real meaning. What is important is what you do with the 18. For example, most teachers would turn it into a percentage indicating that the student got 90 percent (18 ÷ 20 = 90%) on this test.

o *Scaled Scores:* Many tests used for assessment of children have subtests that together compose the entire test. For each subtest, a student receives a raw score. This raw score is often transformed into a scaled score. Scaled scores are very specific subtest scores. In many cases, scaled scores range from 1 to 19 with a mean of 10 and fall into the following classification format:

| Scaled Score | Classification |
|---|---|
| 1–3 | Developmentally delayed |
| 4–5 | Well below average |
| 6–7 | Low average |
| 8–12 | Average |
| 13–14 | High average |
| 15–16 | Superior |
| 17–19 | Very superior |

For example, if a student gets only a scaled score of 7 on a reading subtest but a 13 on a math subtest, this indicates a much greater strength with respect to math than with reading as compared to the norms of that child's age group.

o *Standard Deviation* (abbreviation is *SD*): The standard deviation indicates the amount of variability in a group of scores. When scores are normally distributed (i.e., when they are part of a bell-shaped, "normal" curve), about two-thirds of the scores are within 1 *SD* above and below the average (mean) score, and about 95 percent of scores are within 2 *SDs* of the mean. In almost any shaped distribution, all scores will be within 3 *SDs* of the mean score.

o *Standard Score:* Some tests report scores in what are referred to as Standard Scores. A Standard Score indicates how far a particular score is from a test's average. While it is not important here to get too technical, we have provided the following table for purposes of a rough comparison:

| Standard Score | Classification |
|---|---|
| Less than 70 | Developmentally delayed (This would be a very low score and indicate serious impairment in the particular area.) |
| 70–79 | Well below average or borderline |
| 80–89 | Low average |
| 90–109 | Average |
| 110–119 | High average |
| 120–129 | Superior |
| 130 and higher | Very superior |

For example, if your child receives a Standard Score on a reading test of 115, then your child would be in the above average range of performance. If a Standard Score of 72 was received on a math test, then your child's performance would be very low. However, be aware that some tests may use a different range of standard scores (e.g., Woodcock Johnson).

o *Stanine:* Some scores are reflected in what are called stanines, which stands for *standard nine*. This means that 9 stanines will be used to describe your child's performance from 1–9. Therefore, a stanine of 1, 2, or 3 is usually at the lower levels of performance; 4, 5, and 6 indicate the average range of performance; and stanines of 7, 8, or 9 indicate above average ranges of performance.

o *T Score:* A *T* score is another way to express test performance. *T* scores have a mean of 50 with a standard deviation of 10. Therefore, if you have a *T* score of 40, you are 1 standard deviation below the mean, whereas a *T* score of 60 would be 1 standard deviation above the mean.

o *z Score:* A *z* score indicates how many standard deviations a score is above or below the mean. A *z* score is a standard score distribution with a mean of 0 and a standard deviation of 1. For example, if a student has a *z* score of +1.0, this means that he or she scored 1 standard deviation above the mean on the test. If a student has a *z* score of –1.7, this means that he or she scored 1.7 standard deviations below the mean.

- *Individual education program (IEP):* A very crucial piece of information is the child's most recent individual educational program. Keep in mind that since the reauthorization of IDEA in 2004, there have been many changes to the IEP. However, in general, the IEP will contain the following statements:

o *Present levels of achievement and educational performance.* This statement describes how your student is currently doing in school. This includes how your student's disability affects involvement and progress in the general curriculum.

o *Annual goals.* The IEP must state annual goals for your student, meaning what you and the school team think the student can reasonably accomplish in a year. The goals must relate to meeting the needs that result from your student's disability. They must also help your student be involved in and progress in the general curriculum.

o *Special education and related services to be provided.* The IEP must list the special education and related services to be provided to your student. This includes supplementary aids and services (such as a communication device). It also includes changes to the program or supports for school personnel that will be provided for your student.

o *Participation with nondisabled students.* How much of the school day will your student be educated separately from nondisabled students or not participate in extracurricular or other nonacademic activities, such as lunch or clubs? The IEP must include an explanation that answers this question.

o *Participation in state and districtwide assessments.* Your state and district probably test student achievement in certain grades or age groups. To participate in these tests, your student may need individual modifications or changes in how the tests are administered. The IEP team must decide what modifications your student needs and list them in the IEP. If your student will not be taking these tests, the IEP must include a statement as to why the tests are not appropriate for your student and how your student will be tested instead.

o *Dates and location.* The IEP must state (a) when services and modifications will begin, (b) how often they will be provided, (c) where they will be provided, and (d) how long they will last.

o *Transition goals and services.* No later than when your students are 16, the IEP must include measurable postsecondary goals related to training, education, employment, and (when appropriate) independent living skills. Also included are the transition services needed to help your student reach those goals, including what your student should study.

o *Measuring progress.* The IEP must state how school personnel will measure your student's progress toward the annual goals. It must also state how parents will be informed regularly of their child's progress and whether that progress is enough to enable your student to achieve the stated goals by the end of the year.

- You will need to become very familiar with all the changes under the new law, since you will be involved in writing the child's new IEP at this year's annual review. For more information on the changes in the IEP under IDEA 2004, see the following Web sites:

  National Dissemination Center for Children with Disabilities "NICHCY Connections . . . to Resources on IDEA 2004" (http://nichcy.org/resources/idea2004resources.asp)

  Peter W. D. Wright's "Overview, Explanation and Comparision: IDEA 2004 v. IDEA 97" (www.wrightslaw.com/idea/idea.2004.all.pdf)

- This vital information necessary for learning about your students is usually not found in the permanent record folder. It can normally be obtained from several sources, including the following:
  a. The office of Pupil Personnel Services/Special Education Office
  b. The psychologist's file on the child
  c. The special education folder on the child. This file is normally passed from teacher to teacher. However, this folder may be in a main file in the office of the special education coordinator for your building.

- *Health alerts:* This piece of medical information may be found on the front page of the child's IEP. If something is noted, then it becomes your professional responsibility to learn as much as possible about that health condition. You want to understand the child's health issues. Also, while you are not a medical professional, you will want to sound professional and prepared when you meet with the parent. The parents will feel very reassured when they see that you have an understanding of any conditions that their children may be facing.
- *Classification:* Find out as much as possible about the child's specific disability classification as you can. You may already be knowledgeable about the disability, but it never hurts to learn more. This knowledge base can only gain you respect from staff and parents. Numerous sources on all of the different disability categories can be found through the National Association of Special Education Teachers (www.naset.org).
- *Modifications:* Modifications are adjustments to the child's classroom or test requirements that try to level the "playing field" with nondisabled peers. Look for the classroom and test modifications that the child is entitled to have. These are listed somewhere in the IEP. Investigate each modification thoroughly and fully understand what is involved and the possible rationale for why these were deemed appropriate. You will need to understand these modifications fully, since you will very likely be communicating and explaining them to the child's other teachers.
- *Accommodations:* There may be times when a child is entitled to some classroom accommodation. Examples include special furniture, filters for lighting, acoustic enhancements, etc. Again, investigate and become knowledgeable of each accommodation. The list of accommodations for each student should be clearly described in the IEP.
- *Related services:* The IEP will also contain a section on the related services that the child is entitled to have while in school. The term *related services* means transportation and such developmental, corrective, and other supportive services (including speech-language pathology and audiology services; psychological services; physical and occupational therapy; recreation, including therapeutic recreation; social work services; counseling services, including rehabilitation counseling; orientation and mobility services; and medical services, except that such medical services shall be for diagnostic and evaluation purposes

only) as may be required to assist a child with a disability to benefit from special education, and it includes early identification and assessment of disabling conditions in children. (20 U.S.C. Section 1401(22))

- *Assistive technology:* When looking at your student's IEP, you may notice that some of them are entitled to assistive technology. Assistive technology devices are mechanical aids that substitute for or enhance the function of some physical or mental ability that is impaired. Assistive technology can be anything homemade, purchased off the shelf, modified, or commercially available that is used to help an individual perform some task of daily living. The term *assistive technology* encompasses a broad range of devices from low-tech (e.g., pencil grips, splints, paper stabilizers) to high-tech (e.g., computers, voice synthesizers, Braille readers). These devices include the entire range of supportive tools and equipment, from adapted spoons to wheelchairs and computer systems for environmental control. It will be your responsibility to learn as much as possible about the assistive technology device for each student. A good start in understanding the basics of assistive technology can be found at the University of Buffalo Web site: http://atto.buffalo.edu.
- *Present levels of academic performance:* It is important to determine, if possible, the child's present levels of academic, social, and intellectual ability. These levels, which are measured by many sources, can usually be found in several areas:
  a. *The permanent record folder.* Look for a group IQ test or a test that offers a score labeled "School Abilities Index." These group measures may offer you some insight. Again, be careful about using low scores to determine ability for the same reasons mentioned previously.
  b. *The psychologist's office.* Look up the last triennial report, which should have some measure of ability noted. The triennial evaluation is done every three years. The main purpose of the triennial evaluation is to measure the child's present levels and determine whether the conditions that were used in the original classification are still present.
  c. *The child's IEP.* The IEP may contain an ability level. The child's ability level is usually measured through individual ability tests like the Wechsler Intelligence Scale or the Stanford-Binet Intelligence Scale. The ability levels may be reported as ranges (e.g., average, above average) or as specific scores (e.g., 112, 85). Therefore, you should become

familiar with IQ ranges and within what ranges specific scores may fall. The following table may help you in understanding this issue:

| IQ Score | Percentile | Description |
|----------|------------|-------------|
| 160–169 | 0.03 | Very Superior |
| 150–159 | 0.2 | |
| 140–149 | 1.1 | |
| 130–139 | 3.1 | |
| 120–129 | 8.2 | Superior |
| 110–119 | 18.1 | High Average |
| 100–109 | 23.5 | Normal or Average |
| 90–99 | 23.0 | |
| 80–89 | 14.5 | Low Average |
| 70–79 | 5.6 | Borderline Defective |
| 60–69 | 2.0 | Mentally Defective |
| 50–59 | 0.4 | |
| 40–49 | 0.2 | |
| 30–39 | 0.03 | |

d. *Past teachers' comments about the child's ability levels.* Past teachers' comments can tell you a great deal about patterns of strengths and weaknesses and the history of certain behaviors and academic skill problems. These may be found on past report cards. If they are not, you may want to contact some of the child's past teachers to gather information.

These points should offer you a good beginning in learning as much as possible about your students before school begins. Experience has shown us that the more groundwork you do before school begins, the easier the transition will be for your students and parents.

The next chapter will deal with meeting parents and students before school, as well as meeting with assistant teachers, paraprofessionals, related service providers, classroom teachers, and other professional staff members who will be involved with your students.

# Step II

# Designing and Setting Up Your Classroom

## Part I: Designing the Special Education Classroom

While we do not have much control over which classroom we are assigned as teachers, we do have a great deal of control over how we design and decorate the environment. (Inclusion teachers please see Part II on page 13.) Setting up the physical structure of your classroom is a personal choice. However, some logic should be utilized when determining the layout of the room. In a resource room and self-contained special education classroom, there are several designs that you can consider.

### Station-Oriented Model

A very popular room arrangement involves what is called a station-oriented model. In this model, the room is divided into stations that contain specific content area materials. For example, there might be a reading center, math center, computer center, writing center, and so on, in which specific children go to work on their specific IEP goals. Houghton Mifflin Education Place (2006) lists several different types of learning areas.

### Group Area

This area is utilized for whole-class lessons, including informal discussion, direct instruction, and student presentations. This is a good place for an Author's Chair from which students can read their writing to the class.

### Individual or Small-Group Instruction Area

In this area, you can give small-group instruction or allow groups of students to gather for peer-led discussions. This will be a very important area, since individual or small group instruction is vital to meeting the individual needs of your students.

### Quiet Reading Area

This is a place for students to read independently or quietly with a partner. It should provide comfortable seating, a variety of books, and a quiet, secluded atmosphere.

### Writing Center

Here students write either independently and collaboratively. The area should contain comfortable space for writing and a variety of supplies.

### Computer Area

You will want to separate the computer area from the other areas since this space will be heavily used. Try to keep this area far from any quiet areas since discussion will be common here. This area is for computer use in writing, math, reading, keyboard practice, research, telecommunications, and creative games.

### Creative Arts Area

This area is where students can get involved in visual art and dramatic play. It should have a variety of art supplies, costumes, and props.

### Individual Listening Station

Here students listen to tapes of books, stories, songs, and poems. When setting up your room with a station or learning center approach, take the physical features of your classroom into account when planning. As the school year progresses, you will need to change the type of areas or rearrange them if problems exist in the location or if surrounding areas conflict (e.g., noisy area near quiet area). Keep the following things in mind if you use this type of design:

- Separate learning centers of high activity, such as the cross-curricular center, from areas like the reading/language arts center, where students need quiet.
- Use bookshelves or other types of separation devices to partition off areas.
- Provide comfortable seating by having the children bring in seat cushions.
- Save space by using walls for posters, display shelves, books, and supplies.
- Keep computers facing away from windows to keep glare from sunlight off the screens.
- Set aside an area to meet with small groups. Allow enough seating for about eight students.

### Child-Oriented Model

Some teachers prefer to use a more child-centered model. In this type of setting, the room is arranged so that the children are separated to avoid distraction and increase concentration. Here, the teacher moves from student to student. Since most of the work is individualized, the teacher and the assistant can work on specific limitations for each child with special needs.

### Teacher-Oriented Model

Since there are so many teaching styles, finding your comfort zone will be crucial. In this type of design, the teacher's work table or area is the center of the room. In this way, the teacher can work with several children at a time and monitor their progress. If the teacher feels a child needs less distraction, that student can be moved to another part of the room with or without the assistant teacher.

## Part II: Setting Up Your Inclusion Classroom

While the relationship between teachers is crucial in this type of setting, there may be very little to do, depending on your relationship with the regular education teacher. If you are hired for an elementary inclusion class, the general education teacher may set up the room. However, your input would be helpful, and you may want to ask if the teacher has any concerns about the room design in light of the children with special needs. In this case, assist the teacher, making suggestions if you feel they will better serve the population of children with disabilities (e.g., quiet corner or study carrel to avoid distractions). If you are hired as an inclusion teacher at the high school, then you may have less to do with setting up the room, since many different teachers will be using that room. However, try to assist the teacher and suggest anything that you feel might help.

According to Johnson Smith (2007), there are other issues to consider for setting up your classroom. Some of these include the following:

1. *Check school policies.* Before designing your classroom, ask if there are any school policies that affect classroom displays. For example, some principals require you to post daily objectives, and many schools have fire policies that prohibit hanging paper signs on the door.

2. *Save plenty of space for information.* If you need students to access certain types of information daily, create a consistent space for them to find it. For example, you could post permanent signs at the front of the room that say "Objectives," "Warm-Up Activity," and "Homework" and use the area near these signs to provide details about each. Also, have a space where the date is consistently posted and make sure your name is posted at the beginning of the year.

   Johnson Smith also recommends devoting a section of the room to students who have been absent. If you decide to do this, keep the following tips in mind:
   - Label the space clearly. Have a sign that simply asks "Were you absent?"
   - Hang a calendar nearby to help students identify the day of school they missed.
   - Use a small filing cabinet to house an activity log (listing the work completed each day) and blank copies of all assignments (labeled with titles matching those in the activity log).

   After you introduce students to the space, they become responsible for identifying days they miss, checking the log for work completed on those days, gathering the blank assignments, completing the work, and submitting it to you.

3. *Sticking items on the walls.* The very first thing you will want to do when sticking things on the wall is to make sure the custodian or maintenance person approves the type of adhesive used. Trust me: do this first and get on the good side of these very important people. You may also want to ask your colleagues what adhesives work on the school walls, as some may not stick as long as others. Tape works on some walls, others require putty, and hot glue guns work on the concrete walls in many schools. Finally, you can nail things into the walls. Nails are especially good for holding clipboards (if you want to clip a sign-in sheet near your door) and bathroom passes (if you use anything larger than a paper pass).

4. *Arrange desks with logic and common sense.* Consider your teaching style, class chemistry, management style, and the needs of other teachers when designing the arrangement of the desks. There are several options, and changing the arrangement every several months is a good idea to increase interest and a provide a new atmosphere. Options include rows, clusters, a circle, or some other configuration.

5. *Find alternate ways to gather materials.* Teachers are very resourceful when it comes to saving money and finding alternatives to gather classroom materials. However, a word of caution is called for here. If you are bringing anything into the school, make sure that it is allowed (e.g., small rugs), since some items may be inflammable and not allowed by the fire department. Check with your principal if you are not sure. Keep all your receipts since some schools may reimburse with petty cash. Even if your school does not, you may be able to deduct these as business expenses. Check with your accountant.

6. *Prepare for emergencies.* Locate the emergency call button in your room and learn how to use the intercom system. You don't want to accidentally signify an emergency when you're trying to answer a page from the office on your first day!

7. *Become very organized.* Create your own filing system. You will need places to
   • record and store your lesson plans and resources; and
   • file administrative materials, such as student IEPs, notes from faculty meetings, a parent contact log, discipline log, a faculty handbook, student handbook, hall passes, sub plans, pass codes (for the computers and phones), and important contact numbers.

### Helpful Sites for Information on Setting Up a Classroom

*Inspired Classrooms: "Setting Up a Classroom."* Teacher comments and direction for setting up a classroom (http://inspiredclassrooms .wordpress.com/setting-up-a-classroom/)

*A to Z Teacher Stuff: Forum.* Teacher comments about setting up a classroom (http://forums.atozteacherstuff.com/showthread.php?t= 6501)

*University of Washington's The Faculty Room: "Universal Design of Instruction" by Sheryl Burgstahler, PhD.* Universal design is "the design of products and environments to be usable by all people, to the greatest extent possible, without the need for adaptation or specialized design." (www.washington.edu/doit/Faculty/Strategies/ Universal/)

## Part III: Evaluating Existing Materials

Do not be surprised if when you enter your room for the first time, you find very few materials available for use. You need to hope for the best—and prepare for the worst. In the worst-case scenario, you will need to catalog what is available to you. You should also be able to go to garage sales or elsewhere purchase low-cost items on your own—a reality of teaching. However, be very careful on what you bring into the classroom (e.g., rugs, furniture), since these items may not conform to fire codes of the building. You are safest to consult with your principal first on such items. The checklist in Figure 2.1 might help determine what you have available and what you may need to order.

In summary, the atmosphere of your classroom will go a long way toward minimizing problems and hopefully provide your students with a warm, comfortable, undistracting, and exciting atmosphere in which to work.

**Figure 2.1**     Checklist of Classroom Supplies

*Furniture*

_____Chairs

_____Tables

_____Round table

_____Computer table or cart

_____Bookshelves

_____Blackboard

_____Portable blackboard

_____Book carts

_____Filing cabinets

_____Children's mailboxes or cubbyholes

_____Closets for storage

_____Teacher's desk

_____Teacher's chair

*Classroom Supplies*

_____Writing, drawing, and construction paper

_____Pencils/pens

_____Crayons

_____Paste/glue

_____Stapler/staples

_____Paper clips

_____Rubber bands

_____Straight and safety pins

_____Transparent tape

_____Manila file folders

_____Marking pens

_____Rulers

_____Art supplies

_____Grade book

_____Lesson plan book

_____Attendance materials

_____Textbooks/workbooks

_____Boxes for keeping units

_____Calculator

_____Sticky notes

_____Facial tissues

_____Hole punch

*(Continued)*

**Figure 2.1** (Continued)

_____Pencil sharpener
_____Lined and blank paper
_____Scissors
_____Chalkboard erasers
_____Graph paper in several sizes
_____Pencil grips
_____Markers
_____12″ and 3′ rulers
_____Gummed reinforcements for three-holed paper
_____Pencil erasers
_____Pencil holder
_____Key ring
_____Personal coffee cup or beverage mug
_____5″ × 8″ index cards
_____Hanging files
_____Push tacks
_____Calendar
_____5″ × 8″ legal-ruled writing pads
_____Small screwdriver for glasses repair
_____Safety pins
_____Small sewing kit and tool kit

### Academic Materials

_____Textbooks at several levels
_____Workbooks
_____Worksheets
_____Reading programs
_____Math programs

### Technology

_____Computer
_____Printer
_____Color printer
_____Scanner
_____Cable hookup to the Internet
_____Internet access
_____Word processing program
_____Reading software
_____Math software
_____Spelling software
_____Writing software
_____Voice recognition software and devices
_____Magnification devices

# Step III

# Meeting With Parents and Staff Members

## Part I: Communicating With Parents

Our experience over 30 years of teaching and speaking with thousands of special education teachers has shown that many of the fears of parents may be alleviated by meeting with them before the start of school. This meeting allows you to get to know the parents on a more personal level, allows them to meet you on a more comfortable basis, gives you an opportunity to discuss any fears or concerns, gives you an opportunity to find out their child's interests and strengths, and can break down barriers that come with fear of starting school. However, before we provide practical suggestions for setting up these meetings, we should first talk about conducting positive and effective parent conferences.

### Learn How to Conduct Effective Parent Conferences

As a special educator, you will probably hold parent conferences several times during the school year. A positive conference will tend to influence the parents to be more supportive and involved with their child's work and performance in school. Successful parent conferences also send a positive message to the students that the school and home are working together.

An important skill for special educators is their ability to hold positive parent conferences. Many times, parents will leave a conference having been "bombarded" with jargon and statistics and understand nothing. According to Pierangelo (2004), effectively reporting results of classroom activities, experiences, performance, etc. may be accomplished in the following ways:

1. You will want to make sure that you do not get caught in discussing the issues with the parent on the phone when you go to make the appointment for the conference. Many times, parents' anxiety makes them aggressive in wanting to know everything "right now." However, what you need to do is reassure them that all their concerns and questions will be addressed at the meeting. Just gently say that the type of information that you have is better explained and understood in person. If you sense further anxiety, try to reassure parents that you will meet as soon as possible. It is important to see parents in person so that you can read their body language and further explain areas in which they seem confused or uncomfortable. The face-to-face contact also makes the conference a more human approach. Hearing results from our doctor over the phone may not be as comforting as in person. This is especially true when working with students with learning disabilities, since the parents may already feel a great deal of academic anxiety.

2. Make parents feel comfortable and at ease by setting up a receptive environment. If possible, hold the meeting in a pleasant setting. Whenever possible, use a round table, or any table instead of your desk, and offer some type of refreshment to ease possible tension in the situation.

3. It may be helpful to refresh a parent's memory about the areas on a student's IEP that have been identified as being in need of attention.

4. Go over strength areas first, no matter how few there may be. You can also report positive classroom comments and any other information that may help set the tone for acceptance of problem areas.

5. Provide a typed outline of any classroom test scores, grades, and group achievement test results for the parent to take home. It looks more professional if this information is typed, and having a copy in hand may alleviate potential problems that parents encounter when sharing the information with their spouses or partners.

6. It is strongly suggested that you provide a key to any potentially confusing terminology that may be communicated to parents. If you are discussing test results, for example, explain in simple terms any statistical terms you may be using (e.g., percentiles, stanines, standard scores, etc.). In fact, it may be a good idea to define these in writing on the same sheet with the scores so that parents have a key when they review them at home.

7. Often parents will try to memorize the entire parent conference, but of course, memory is notorious faulty. Much of what is actually said may be communicated erroneously to another parent/stepparent who did not attend the meeting. Therefore, it is wise to offer parents a pad and pen so that they can write down information, terms, or reactions during the meeting. Further, let them know that they should feel free to call you with any questions or concerns that may arise after they go home.

8. When you plan the conference, make sure that you leave yourself enough time for issues that might arise out of the parent's anxiety, particularly if you foresee the conference will be difficult. Challenging conferences are not ones in which you want to run out of time. The parents should leave in a natural manner, rather than feeling rushed.

9. Take time to explain the differences between *symptoms* and *problems*. This explanation can go a long way in alleviating a parent's frustration. Parents need to understand that behaviors like avoidance, procrastination, resistance, difficulty getting started with homework, incomplete assignments, etc. may be symptoms of a problem (e.g., learning disability, fear of failure, fear of disappointment, fear of criticism).

10. It is helpful for parents to hear how the problems or areas of concern you found were contributing to the symptoms in the classroom and at home. It is reassuring for parents to know that what they were seeing were only symptoms, even though they may have been quite intense, and that the problems have been identified and recommendations are available. Offer them as much realistic hope as possible by giving them a plan of what you will attempt to do to remediate the weaknesses and what they can do at home to help.

11. Be as practical and specific as possible when offering suggestions for how parents can help at home. Offer them printed

sheets with step-by-step procedures for any recommendation that you make. Parents should not be expected to be teachers and should never be given general recommendations that require their interpretation (e.g., "provide positive reinforcement"). Such vague guidance may aggravate an already tense situation at home. Offer them supportive and educational materials that they can use with their child, providing them insight into how they can create success.

## Communicating With Parents for Primary Inclusion Teachers

If you can begin this process a week before school, then consider sending home a letter to parents introducing yourself and inviting them in just to see the room and so you can get to know each other. However, you will want to make sure that your classroom is set up so that parents get a good feeling of organization and comfort. Keep these meetings very informal. Following are some examples of introductory letters you might send.

*From a New Teacher*

---

Dear _____:

    I would like to take this opportunity to introduce myself as your child's new (Resource Room, Inclusion, Special Class) teacher for the coming school year. My name is _____, and I am very excited about being at the _____School. My background includes _____. I was hired this year to teach this class and look forward to working very closely with you so that (child's name) can have a very rewarding and productive year.

    To get to know one another, I am inviting the parent(s) of my students in for an informal get-together. I have set aside several dates and times so that I can meet with parent(s) separately. Please give me a call so that I can reserve a time for you to come in and see the room, meet with me, and talk about the exciting things we will be doing this year.

    I look forward to hearing from you.

Sincerely yours,

---

*From an Experienced Teacher*

---

Dear _____:

I would like to take this opportunity to introduce myself as your child's new (Resource Room, Inclusion, Special Class) teacher for the coming school year. My name is _____, and I am very excited about having taught at the _____School for _____ years. I look forward to working very closely with you so that (child's name) can have a very rewarding and productive year.

To get to know one another, I am inviting the parent(s) of my students in for an informal get-together. I have set aside several dates and times so that I can meet with parent(s) separately. Please give me a call so that I can reserve a time for you to come in and see the room, meet with me, and talk about the exciting things we will be doing this year.

I look forward to hearing from you.

Sincerely yours,

---

On the elementary level, you may want to invite parents to meet with you individually and then, sometime in late September, hold a group meeting for all parents. You should consider meeting individually first, in case there is a parent that is very angry at the system, school, etc. You do not want to take the chance that this parent might use the group meeting as a platform for personal issues. Also, you do not want Open School Night to be the first time you meet an angry parent. By meeting with each parent first, you may be able to reassure the parent or defuse any concerns. Since elementary educational settings will have smaller numbers of children, this type of plan should be realistic.

When you meet with the parents, you should discuss the following issues so that everyone is clear about their roles and responsibilities:

- Parent roles and responsibilities
- Parental expectations
- Parent involvement with homework
- Communication between home and school and between school and home

At this meeting, you will want to speak with each parent and get a sense of his concerns, fears, questions, or insight concerning his child. You can learn a great deal from parents about the child's likes and dislikes, triggers, unstructured behavior patterns, hobbies, areas of interests, athletic abilities, pets, and anything else that might contribute to forming a future bond between you and the child.

## Communicating With Parents for Secondary Inclusion Teachers

A secondary-level inclusion classroom normally does not lend itself to individual meetings, because teachers in this setting work with class totals on any given day of over 100 students, both with and without disabilities. However, communication with the parents of children with disabilities is still necessary. You, as the teacher, may still want to send home an introductory letter but not suggest individual meetings prior to school. In these cases, you may want to learn more about each child from her parent through an enclosed questionnaire, checklist, or both. Friend & Bursuck (2005) provides the following series of questions, which might serve as a structure for such questionnaires or checklists:

a. What is your child's favorite class activity?

b. Does your child have any worries about class activities? If so, what are they?

c. What are your priorities for your child's education this year?

d. What questions do you have about your child's education in my class this year?

e. How could we at school make this the most successful year ever for your child?

f. Are there any topics you want to discuss that may require a conference? If so, please let me know.

g. If a conference is requested, would you like other individuals to participate? If so, please give me a list of their names so that I can invite them.

h. If a conference is requested, would you like me to have particular school information available? If so, please let me know.

i. If you have any questions that I may be able to answer by phone, you can reach me (between 7:30 and 8:10 AM and between 3:00 and 3:30 PM) at (phone number). If you prefer, you can reach me by e-mail at _____.

In your initial letter, you should address the same issues indicated above for the other settings:

- Parent roles and responsibilities
- Parental expectations
- Parent involvement with homework
- Communication between home and school and between school and home

## Part II: Meeting With Your Assistant Teacher or Aide Before School Begins (Special Education Class)

Many special education teachers work with one or more paraprofessionals, aides, or assistant teachers to help them, depending on the level of severity of the student population. The best way to get the most from these assistants is by encouraging them to take responsibility for getting results in the classroom. To do this, you need to involve them in almost every phase of the classroom—supervision, planning, grading, record keeping, and teaching, to name a few. Keep in mind that the level of responsibilities will vary for all three positions; aide, paraprofessional, and assistant teacher, depending on their training and job description. Try to get a copy of the job description from central administration or the principal. This is usually put together when hiring for a position. The job description will provide an excellent starting place for discussion and expectations. Keep the following general suggestions in mind when working with paraprofessionals, aides, or assistant teachers in your classroom:

1. Find out about their abilities and talents so that you can draw on them during the school year.

2. Foster an environment where they can make and try suggestions. At the same time, you must let it be known that you are in charge and will make the final decision. After all, you will be the one to take responsibility if something goes wrong, so make sure all suggestions go through you before the assistant puts them into action. Also, keep in mind that if you feel your assistant is not using good judgment, you may have to play a more authoritarian role by having ideas passed by you first. The assistant should understand the reasoning behind this, since you will be the one called if something goes wrong.

3. Foster a team approach where everyone is vital to a successful outcome. Let them see that you appreciate initiative. Make sure they realize that they are essential to the success of the students with whom they work.

4. While you will want to make it clear that you are always in charge and everything will need to go through you, you may want to treat your assistant as a "second teacher" in the classroom. Train him or her in observation of learning styles and behavioral symptoms that may indicate other issues (e.g., distractibility, impulsivity) and to see what needs to be done and do it. However, be very aware that liability issues may arise if the children are left with an aide, paraprofessional, or assistant teacher who is not a licensed certified teacher. If a child gets hurt or problems arise while you are not in the room, there could be problems. Meet with your supervisor and discuss this matter to determine your guidelines and responsibilities in these cases (Pierangelo, 2004).

5. Make the aide, paraprofessional, or assistant teacher aware of the IEP goals for each student. These individuals will acquire personal growth when you trust them and appreciate what they do.

6. Short written notes of thanks are a really good practice. These include such statements as "I want to thank you for being so positive when talking to the students."

7. First-year teachers seem very unsure of how to use their aides. If aides are idle, resources are being underutilized. At first, you may have to organize and instruct the aide on what to do. Do not be afraid to be highly structured and direct. This will alleviate the anxiety of the inexperienced aide and provide needed guidance.

8. Aides and teaching assistants perform numerous duties, including assisting with grading and duplicating worksheets. Do not be afraid to allow them to handle tasks that will free up your time for more critical matters, such as working with your students. However, working with students, whether individually or in small groups, is their most important function.

9. If problems arise with your aide, paraprofessional, or assistant, you may want to meet with the school psychologist, your coordinator of special education, or the principal to determine a way to resolve the issues. It is advisable to act promptly in these instances—the longer you wait to talk about a challenging situation, the more difficult it often becomes.

## Meet With Your Inclusion
## Team Teacher (Inclusion Class)

The relationship between the special education teacher and the regular education teacher in an inclusion setting is crucial to the success of the program. Many schools provide workshops and ongoing seminars that provide ongoing training for the teachers involved. A quality inservice program must afford faculty and staff experiences for continually upgrading their skills to support increasingly more inclusive learning communities (Villa, Thousand, & Chapple, 1996). Many questions and issues need to be discussed to prevent misconceptions, frustration, or dissension. To avoid potential issues, the following suggestions should be considered:

- Discuss the specifics of your roles and clearly define your professional responsibilities so that there is no confusion during class time. Make sure that your responsibilities are not defined so that the class is split in two (i.e., you taking care of the discipline and academic needs of children with special needs and the regular education teacher dealing only with the mainstream population). This would be tragically counterproductive to the goal of inclusion.
- Discuss the similarities and differences in each other's teaching styles and how they might affect the students and the presentation of information. Even if your teaching styles are different, they can complement each other.
- Discuss the various delivery systems options to determine which ones are most comfortable. There are several different teaching methods for instruction and assistance of children in an inclusion setting, referred to as alternative delivery systems. These are management systems that provide support for students and maximize learning while being presented with the core curriculum in an inclusion setting.

According to Center for Innovations in Education (Wunder & Lindsey, 2006), there are five models of cooperative teaching: complementary instruction, station teaching, parallel teaching, alternative teaching, and team teaching:

- *Complementary instruction.* Complementary instruction blends the general and special education teacher roles. Both educators are in the same room at the same time. However, one teacher assumes the roles of lead teacher while the other circulates the room, observes, and provides assistance as necessary. Two applications of the complementary instructional model most frequently demonstrated in practice are one teach/one observe and one teach/one assist.

o *One teach/one observe.* With one teach/one observe, one of the partners observes the classroom to gather relevant data while the other partner instructs. The observer can compile anecdotal information, record feedback concerning the effectiveness of the classroom management, or maintain records of individual students' and the class's time on task. To facilitate the students' perception of both as teachers, the observer's role and the lead teacher's role should be rotated.

o *One teach/one assist.* With one teach/one assist, the instruction expertise of the special educator and the general educator are combined. The general education teacher is the content specialist in the specific subject. Instructional responsibilities include the scope and sequences of the curriculum, grading projects and tests, and assigning the grade for the course. The special education teacher is the academic skill strategist. Instructional responsibilities include the instruction of academic survival skills and learning strategies that the students need for learning the core curriculum.

• *Station teaching instruction.* Station teaching instruction is divided into two or three parts, and each teacher presents a lesson at one station through which students rotate. At each station, one teacher provides half the instructional content. In some instances, a third station where students can work independently may be appropriate. Lessons using this method must not be dependent on the order of the content presented, as groups of students will progress through the stations in different order.

• *Parallel teaching.* During parallel teaching, both teachers present the same content to one half of the class simultaneously. This model works best when student response (discussion) is required or instruction involves hands-on activities.

• *Alternative teaching.* During alternative teaching, one teacher instructs a small group of students apart from the rest of the class. The purpose of this grouping may be for enrichment, reteaching, preteaching, special projects, makeup material, assessment, or teaching social skills. All students should be allowed to take advantage of this method, and heterogeneous grouping should be maintained.

- *Team teaching.* Team teaching is when both teachers simultaneously share the direct instruction of the content. This method requires more planning but allows teachers to blend their styles and expertise.

## Part III: Communicating With Related-Service Providers (All Settings)

In general, the final regulations for IDEA 2004 define the term *related services* as "transportation and such developmental, corrective, and other supportive services as are required to assist a child with a disability to benefit from special education." The following are included within the definition of related services:

- Speech-language pathology and audiology services
- Psychological services
- Physical and occupational therapy
- Recreation, including therapeutic recreation
- Early identification and assessment of disabilities in children
- Counseling services, including rehabilitation counseling
- Orientation and mobility services
- Medical services for diagnostic or evaluation purposes
- School health services
- Social work services in schools
- Parent counseling and training
- Transportation

When one of your students has been identified on the IEP as requiring related services, it will be your responsibility to coordinate the services with these providers. Therefore, it is very important that you maintain close communication with every related-service provider involved with the students in your classroom. These professionals will provide related services to your students on a regular basis throughout the school year. You will want to maintain the most up-to-date information in case you are questioned by parents, students, or administrators. To set up these lines of communication, initiate the following steps:

1. Send out letters to the related-service providers for each child, introducing yourself and asking for a time to get together. Outline the objectives of such a meeting, including coordination of services, avoiding scheduling conflicts, communication, and IEP development. An example of this type of letter follows:

---

**Letter to Related-Service Provider**

Dear _____:

    During this school year, I will be (child's first and last name)'s special education teacher. It is noted on (child's name)'s IEP that he or she is to receive (related service) (frequency; i.e., 1 × week) from you beginning on (date; as close to the start of school as possible). To coordinate services, I am suggesting that we get together for a meeting to discuss schedules, communication with parents and teachers, modifications and accommodations, and any other matters that may assist (child's name) this year.

    I will try to contact you to see what times and days are convenient for you, or if you prefer, I can be reached at (phone and extension) between the hours of_____. My room number is _____at the (name of school) school.

    I look forward to meeting with you.

Sincerely yours,

---

2. After the letter is sent, seek out the related-service provider and set up a meeting. At this meeting, discuss schedules, goals of the service, expectations, communication with parents, and collaboration meetings to discuss the child's progress.

3. If you are designated the case manager, the designee responsible for coordinating the child's IEP, discuss the means for communicating information that will be necessary in developing the new IEP at the annual review meeting.

4. Also find out as much as you can about the child's specific problem, etiology (cause) and prognosis (outcome) from the service provider.

# Part IV: Communicating With Your Student's Regular Education Teachers (Resource Room Teachers)

If you are teaching in a resource room, your students will be mainstreaming in a regular education class most of the day. (Self-contained teachers please see Part V on page 32.) One of your most important responsibilities, after assisting children, is working in coordination with the classroom teachers. Most likely, your major role with the child's classroom teacher will be to

- assist in adapting curriculum;
- monitor modifications;
- prepare adapted materials for the child to use in the classroom;
- provide information and suggestions on the child's disability; and
- provide alternate curriculum materials suited to the child's skill levels.

The first thing to consider doing if you are a new special education teacher is to place a letter in the teacher's mailbox introducing yourself, offering some background information, and listing the name(s) of the children you wish to discuss. Indicate in the letter that you will contact the teacher to set up a convenient time to meet to discuss any issues pertaining to the children receiving resource room services. If this is not your first year, then adapt the letter accordingly. An example of this type of letter follows:

---

**Classroom Teacher Letter: First-Year Teacher**

Dear _____:

My name is _____, and this school year I will be working with (first and last name of child), a student in your class. (Child's first name) has been assigned this service according to her IEP (designate the period for services). These services are being provided to her for the following reasons:

(State reasons—usually weakness areas determined by an evaluation or IEP team.)

To collaborate on providing these services, I would like to meet with you to discuss (child's first name)'s program, scheduling time, parent communication, and modifications that are required as a result of her IEP. I will be stopping by your room to discuss a convenient time for this meeting and look forward to speaking with you, or if you prefer, I can be reached at (phone and extension) between the hours of_____. My room number is _____.

I look forward to meeting with you.

Sincerely yours,

---

During this personal meeting with the child's classroom teacher, you will want to cover several objectives:

- Try to determine your responsibilities and the resources you can provide to the teacher (e.g., adapting the curriculum, links and resource information on the disability, finding suitable materials for the child's skill levels).
- Determine a realistic and practical schedule for the child that limits stress and avoids the possibility of fragmentation. Fragmentation occurs when a child leaves the classroom to go to the resource room in the middle of one lesson and returns in the middle of another. Fragmentation can be detrimental to a child who is already confused by the demands of the curriculum. Try to find a convenient time that will ease the transition for the child to and from the room.
- Provide the child's classroom and test modifications outlined on the IEP to the classroom teacher. Provide the classroom teacher with a written statement of these modifications. Discuss how they should be implemented in the classroom. Make sure that you get this letter back for your files with the signature of the teacher indicating that you have made the teacher aware of the requirements of the modifications and accommodations. This signed letter will protect you in case you are accused of not informing staff members of the child's modification needs.
- Discuss fully the child's IEP step-by-step so that the teacher is cognizant of what has been determined by the IEP committee.
- Discuss any curriculum concerns that the teacher may have and offer alternatives and options.
- Talk about how to coordinate parent communication. Discuss how often to hold parent meetings or send home communication (e.g., progress reports) and what kind of communication will be reported to parents.
- Listen to the teacher for concerns and fears and try to alleviate them with practical suggestions and the promise of assistance.

## Part V: Communicating With the Mainstreaming Team and Classroom Teachers (Self-Contained Class)

As a teacher in a self-contained class or special education class, you will be faced with the important decision of whether or not to mainstream some of your students into regular education classes. Keep in mind that mainstreaming can be anywhere from five minutes to five hours or more, depending upon the needs and abilities of the child. If mainstreaming is your goal, then the first thing to do is to set up a preliminary meeting with the mainstreaming team in your school. This team is responsible for the process involved in mainstreaming a student to the regular education setting. The mainstreaming team is usually made up of professionals in the school (e.g., school psychologist, general education teacher, special education teacher), the parent, and the student. This may be a formal team or a team that is gathered to discuss these issues on an as-needed basis. If the team agrees with mainstreaming, you will need to do several things to prepare the regular education teacher. As a result, you will want to be ready to discuss the following:

- Why you feel the child is ready for mainstreaming
- The child's areas of strengths that will enhance his experience by being mainstreamed
- The learning style of the child
- The teaching style that will best serve the needs of this student
- The length of time for mainstreaming and the specific subject or social area being suggested

Once the decision has been discussed and a date set for the mainstreaming process to begin, meet with the assigned teacher and offer the following:

- Specific information on the child's disability as well as Internet sites and names of books or articles the teacher may want to research
- Adaptive materials that could be used in the classroom to increase the child's chances of completion and success and to avoid frustration
- Suitable materials for the child's skill levels
- Suggestions for monitoring progress. Discuss specific goals (e.g., academic, behavioral, social, and emotional goals) that you may have for the child and how you will go about determining whether the situation is working for the child and/or the teacher.
- Your role in meeting with the student before and after the mainstreaming experience
- A schedule of meetings with the general education teacher on a regular basis to answer any questions and resolve any issues that need to be addressed

- The child's classroom and test modifications outlined on the IEP. Discuss how these should be implemented in the classroom and leave the teacher with a written statement of these modifications.
- Go over the child's IEP step-by-step so that the teacher is fully aware of what has been determined by the IEP team. (Depending on the state in which you work, this team may also be referred to as the "eligibility committee" or the "committee on special education.")
- Coordination of parent communication. Discuss how often to hold parent meetings or send home communication (e.g., progress reports) and what kind of communication will be reported to parents.

In conclusion, the more interaction and communication you have with parents and staff members, the greater chance you have of avoiding misconceptions, anger, miscommunication, and resentment. This type of communication, with its accompanying paper record of meetings and information exchanged, will also protect you against issues of liability should a problem arise.

# Step IV

# Factors Affecting Curriculum Performance for Students With Special Needs

As a general education teacher working with students with special needs, you will be heavily involved in teaching curriculum. It is therefore important that you understand the many factors that may sometimes interfere in the ability of these students to perform up to their ability while in school. Children are faced with many pressures every day, and these pressures may play a role in their ability to concentrate fully in school. What you notice as a general education teacher may only be symptoms of these pressures (e.g., procrastination, avoidance, resistance, lack of completion of a task, lack of attention, etc.). However, you should know the real reasons behind these behaviors so that you can, along with the special education teacher, make accommodations or adaptations to the curriculum to help these students succeed. This chapter will inform you of the eight factors that contribute to problems in curriculum performance by students with special needs.

# Factors Affecting Curriculum

Children and adults are exposed to a variety of stressors on any given day. For children, these stressors may manifest themselves in school-related symptoms that result in dysfunction. All problems create tension. This tension must be relieved either verbally or behaviorally. If a child is unable to communicate his feelings, as is the case for most children, then that tension will exhibit itself in symptomatic behavior. This symptomatic behavior is what teachers see every day in the classroom. While symptoms themselves do not always indicate whether a serious problem is present, the frequency, intensity, and duration of the symptoms usually do.

Teachers are confronted with symptomatic behavior every day. If they do not understand the nature of the symptoms, they will treat them as problems. Treating a fever as a problem will never cure the infection. While it is true that teachers need not "cure" the problem, it is important that they recognize symptom patterns of more serious conditions so that the proper referrals can be made.

If a teacher understands the nature of symptomatic behavior and makes the proper referral for guidance, then a more serious problem can be averted. However, even if correctly identified, a child's symptomatic behavior may take awhile to dissipate. During this time, teachers can use certain techniques that may calm the child, provide suitable boundaries, reduce classroom frustration, and so on while the real problem is being resolved.

However, before addressing these techniques, we will discuss eight factors that can contribute stress in a child's life. Any of these factors, if intense enough, can create classroom symptoms resulting in academic, behavioral, or social dysfunction.

## Academic Factors

There will always be times when academic deficits will impair a child's ability to function in the classroom. These deficits will make it hard for the child to keep up with the other students and may require added time to complete tasks. Further, a lack of academic skills may cause resistance and opposition to learning. Knowing what is behind resistance may make it easier to overcome it. Factors that can contribute to academic dysfunction include but are not limited to the following:

- Developmental math disorders, sometimes referred to as dyscalculia
- Developmental reading disorders, sometimes referred to as dyslexia
- Developmental spelling disorders, sometimes referred to as dysorthographia
- Developmental writing disorders, sometimes referred to as dysgraphia
- Inconsistency during critical periods of skill development because the child was deprived of learning at critical stages of development
- Lack of basic skills, resulting in the child's being still at the representational level (thinking level) rather than the automatic level, which speeds up processing and performance
- Lack of reinforcement, because the child did not have any significant others who reinforced learning or the need for school performance.
- Poor prior teaching, because the child was exposed to poor-quality teaching or schools

## Environmental Factors

Students have lives outside of school, and all too often, these lives are filled with turmoil, chaos, and dysfunction. Exposure to these factors drains a child of her energy, making it harder to concentrate and attend while in school. After all, children who may experience violence in the home are more worried about going home after school then concentrating on math problems. Environmental factors are defined as those factors to which the child may be exposed at home or in the community that may have a profound impact on the child's ability to function in school. These factors may include the following home issues:

- Alcoholism
- Divorce
- Drug abuse
- Economic hardship
- Family physical illness
- Family mental illness
- Loss of parent's job
- Moving into a new neighborhood

- Parental abuse
- Parenting fighting
- Relatives residing in the home
- Separation
- Serious sibling rivalry

Environmental factors may also originate from community issues:

- Problems with neighbors
- Poor reputation in the neighborhood
- Isolation of the family from neighbors
- Problems with the law

### Intellectual Factors

A child's difficulties in school may be the result of intellectual factors. While a child's ability may vary, it is imperative that as a teacher you have a good idea of each child's true ability level so that you do not frustrate him and you can adapt the curriculum to his needs. When intellectual factors are present, a child's stress may be manifested in a variety of symptoms. The factors that fall under this category include the following:

- Undetected limited intellectual ability
- Undetected gifted intellectual capacity

### Language Factors

With so many children coming from other countries and not being able to speak English, language ability may play a dominant role in a child's ability to perform in school. Further, other children may have language-processing problems even if they are not from another country. Regardless of the source, you will need to be aware of how this factor affects the performance of children in the classroom. Language provides the foundation upon which communication; problem solving; and integrating, analyzing, and synthesizing knowledge takes place. Therefore, deficits in language can have a profound impact on an individual's ability to learn and function competently and confidently as he interacts in the world.

Difficulties in a child's language development that may result in classroom symptoms include the following:

- *Aphasia (dysphasia):* This language problem is caused by brain damage, usually in the left side of the brain. Dysphasia is characterized by a complete or partial loss of ability to understand, speak, read, or write.
- *Articulation disorder:* This problem is characterized by the inability to produce individual speech sounds clearly and difficulty combining sounds correctly for words.
- *Bilingualism:* This term has varying definitions, ranging from perfect command of two languages to the ability to use a second language in however limited a way for practical purposes.
- *Expressive language disorder:* Some children have problems expressing themselves in speech. For example, a child who often calls objects by the wrong names has an expressive language disorder.
- *Problems in phonological awareness:* Phonological awareness is a person's explicit knowledge of the sound segments (phonemes) that comprise words. Phonological processing skills include the ability to recognize and produce rhyming words or patterns of alliteration, segmenting or breaking apart words into syllables/ sounds, identifying where a specific sound occurs in a word, and blending sounds into words.
- *Pragmatic language:* This refers to using language for a specific purpose, such as asking for help.
- *Receptive language disorder.* A child with this disorder has trouble understanding certain aspects of speech even though the child's hearing is fine.
- *Semantic-pragmatic disorder: Semantics* concerns what words mean and how words relate to each other. *Pragmatics* concern the understanding of unspoken conversational rules and hidden meaning in language. Children with semantic-pragmatic difficulties are often able to make sentences but find it difficult to use them appropriately.

## Medical Factors

Numerous medical factors may contribute to a child's academic dysfunction. While teachers are not asked to be doctors, some medical conditions may manifest through certain symptoms in the classroom. For the most part, one would assume that any serious medical condition would have already been identified by the child's pediatrician or parent. However, this may not always be the case, especially in the case of very young children. More common medical problems that may impair a child's ability to function adequately in the classroom include, but are not limited to, the following:

- Attention deficit disorder
- Coordination problems
- Hearing problems
- Muscular problems
- Neurological problems
- Vision problems

## Perceptual Factors

Perceptual issues can impair a child's ability to function in the classroom. While perceptual deficits are often misunderstood or undiagnosed, they do account for a large number of high-risk children. Being able to identify the symptoms of serious perceptual deficits can only reduce a child's frustration, both in and out of the classroom. Perception is a process that involves many different areas. While most of us take it for granted, for some children, it represents a very difficult, frustrating, and deflating experience.

The learning process is like an assembly line through which information travels. Information is received in some manner and is filtered through a series of psychological processes. As information progresses along this "assembly line," it is given meaning and organized in some fashion, then expressed through a variety of responses. When we evaluate a child's perceptual abilities, we are looking to see if a deficit in some area of the learning process may be slowing down the processing of information, thereby interfering in the child's ability to receive, organize, memorize, or express information. Severe deficits in the learning process can have adverse affects upon a child's academic performance.

It is therefore imperative that teachers and other professionals identify as soon as possible those perceptual factors that may impede a child's ability to process information, possibly interfering in her academic achievement.

## Psychological Factors

Tension is present in many children, and the greater the tension, the greater the impact on a child's ability to learn. As tension rises, it affects a child's ability to concentrate, focus, remember and store information, participate, keep things in perspective, and remain patient. As tension goes up, so may distractibility, impulsivity, and avoidance, since all of these factors require energy that is being drained by tension. Psychological factors that may contribute to a child's dysfunction in school may include, but are not limited, to the following:

- *Anxiety:* Apprehension, tension, or uneasiness from anticipation of danger, the source of which is largely unknown or unrecognized
- *Brief situational disturbances or adjustment reactions:* An imprecise term referring to emotional or behavioral symptoms that develop in response to an identifiable stressor
- *Conduct disorders:* A disruptive behavior disorder of childhood characterized by repetitive and persistent violation of the rights of others or of age-appropriate social norms or rules
- *Depression:* A symptom of a variety of mental or physical disorders, a syndrome of associated symptoms secondary to an underlying disorder, or a specific mental disorder
- *Eating disorders:* Marked disturbance in eating behavior
- *Obsessive-compulsive disorders:* An anxiety disorder in which the mind is flooded with persistent and uncontrollable thoughts (obsessions) or the individual is compelled to repeat certain acts again and again in a ritualistic fashion (compulsions), causing significant distress and interference with everyday functioning
- *Oppositional defiant disorders:* Syndrome of chronic misbehavior in childhood marked by belligerence, irritability, and defiance, although not to the extent found in a diagnosis of conduct disorder
- *Personality disorders:* Chronic pattern of maladaptive cognition, emotion, and behavior that begins in adolescence or early adulthood and continues into later life
- *Schizophrenia:* A functional psychosis, of which there are several diagnostic types, characterized by apathy, withdrawal from reality, excessive fantasy, and in some cases delusions and hallucinations
- *Separation anxiety:* The normal fear and apprehension noted in infants when they are removed from the mother (or surrogate mother) or when approached by strangers, most marked from age 6 to 10 months; in later life, similar reactions caused by separation from significant persons or familiar surroundings
- *Substance abuse:* Diagnosis given when a person's recurrent substance use leads to significant harmful consequences, as

manifested by a failure to fulfill obligations at work, school, or home; the use of substances in physically hazardous situations; legal problems; and continued use despite social and legal problems

## Social Factors

Social factors may contribute to a child's stress and consequently interfere with learning. While social status is a crucial factor at many ages, it becomes more of a factor as one approaches adolescence. Social pressures and peer influence sometimes create an imbalance in a child's functioning. This imbalance may often result in lower available energy for school-related issues because of the intense need for energy to cope with the social world or social conflicts. Social factors that may lower available energy and result in academic dysfunction include the following:

- Low social status
- Peer competition
- Peer rejection
- Preoccupation with boyfriend or girlfriend
- Scapegoat
- Social control issues, the need to be in control
- Social intimidation
- Social isolation
- Social overindulgence
- Social victimization
- Victim of bullying behavior

It would be helpful at the beginning of the semester to try to determine which of these areas affects each of your students. Once you have determined this, you may need assistance from other staff members to help the student.

# Step V

# Adapting the Curriculum for Students With Special Needs

One of the most important things to keep in mind when working with students with special needs is that they can learn. In many cases, it is not the lack of understanding or knowledge that causes problems but rather the manner of presentation, response requirements, and level of presentation. Learning how to adapt material is crucial when working with this population. These adaptations offer students a better chance of success and task completion.

## What Are Curriculum Adaptations?

You will need to consider several factors in adapting the curriculum. Adaptive instructional programs are characterized by combined teaching strategies, flexible scheduling, individualized instruction, mastery learning, large- and small-group instruction, individualized tutorials, and cooperative learning. Further, while we need to adapt the form of instruction to meet children's individual needs, we also need to adapt the delivery and response factors that face the child in school.

## Examples of Curriculum Adaptation

Where a student with special needs is expected to achieve or surpass the learning outcomes set out in the science curriculum, regular grading practices and reporting procedures are followed. For students not expected to achieve the learning outcomes, adaptations and modifications must be noted in the Individual Education Plan. In this way, instructional and assessment methods may be adapted to meet the needs of all students.

Following are examples of adaptations that may assist students with special needs achieve success in science.

### Environmental Adaptations

- Separate the classroom into different stations, as previously mentioned.
- Change where the student sits in the classroom.
- Make use of cooperative grouping.

### Presentation of Material

- Provide students with advance organizers of key scientific concepts.
- Demonstrate or model new concepts.

### Pace of Activities

- Allow the student more time to complete assignments.
- Provide shorter but more frequent assignments.

### Alternate Methods of Response and Outcomes

- Build models.
- Cut and paste.
- Cut pictures from magazines.
- Dictate to a scribe.
- Draw pictures.
- Enlarge/shrink materials.
- Use a calculator.
- Use the computer.
- Use manipulatives.
- Use overlays/acetate on text pages.
- Use a tape recorder.

## Adapt Materials

- Cover parts of worksheets.
- Highlight key points on the activity sheet.
- Highlight or color-code (directions, key words, topic sentences).
- Make sections on paper (e.g., draw lines, fold).
- Provide more white space to put answers.
- Put less information on a page.
- Use different types of paper (e.g., graph, paper with midlines, raised-line paper).
- Use high-contrast colors.
- Use large-print activity sheets.
- Use line indicators.
- Use overlays on text pages to reduce the quantity of print that is visible.

## Assistance to Students

- Use peers or volunteers to assist students with special needs.
- Use students with special needs to assist younger students in learning science.
- Use teacher assistants to work with small groups of students, as well as with an identified student with special needs.
- Use consultants and support teachers for problem solving and to assist in developing strategies for science instruction.

## Assessing Student Progress

- Allow various ways for students to demonstrate their understanding of scientific concepts, such as performing experiments, creating displays and models, and tape-recording observations.
- Adapt assessment tools such as paper-and-pencil tests to include options such as oral tests, open-book tests, and tests with no time limit.
- Keep work samples on carbonless copy paper.
- Use computer programs that provide opportunities for scientific practice and recording results.
- Provide opportunities for extension and practice.
- Require small amounts of work to be completed at a given time.
- Simplify the way questions are worded to match the student's level of understanding.

- Provide functional everyday examples, such as building structures to develop an understanding of forces (British Columbia Ministry of Education, Special Education Services, 2006).

## Ways to Adapt the Curriculum

ORCLISH, a statewide, federally funded project under the direction of the Ohio Department of Education's Division of Special Education, put together a checklist of suggestions for adapting instruction. This checklist offers specific areas on which to focus when you work with your students with special needs.

### What to Adapt?

- Classroom organization and behavior management (daily schedules and routines, classroom rules, seating arrangements, and individualized behavior plans)
- Curriculum materials (textbook assignments, workbook, tests)
- Instruction (grouping strategies, learning centers, audiovisuals)

Consider these areas, as well as others, and consider adaptations in several areas at one time to maximize results.

### Alternate Goals

Change the expected outcome or goal for the student while using the same materials or curriculum as other students. For example, the student will only copy the spelling words while others will spell from memory; the student will match state names to the map while others will locate state capitals; or the student will build the DNA model while others build the model, label it, and answer questions.

### Substitute Curriculum

Provide different instruction, materials, and goals for a student. For example, a student may learn computer/keyboarding skills while others are taking a language test; a student may cut out food items from a magazine and create a picture book of favorite foods while others are writing a creative story; a student will create a personal schedule for the day while others are doing group circle or calendar time.

## Staying On Task

- Break assignments down into small units.
- Lessen homework expectations (if necessary).
- Provide frequent teacher feedback and redirection.
- Provide time in resource room for completion of class work.
- Use a buddy system to remind child to stay on task.

## Homework

- Allow more time.
- Individualize.
- Provide more help.
- Shorten.

## Presentation of Material

- Divide instruction into small steps.
- Present visually (e.g., writing, demonstration, pictures, objects, computers, videos, maps, charts, calendars, audiotapes)
- Provide needed prompts and cues.
- Provide opportunities to teach and practice skills needed.

## Assessment and Assignments

- Allow extra time.
- Alter activity.
- Highlight text.
- Link learning to real situations.
- Modify difficulty.
- Modify question format.
- Provide a choice (when appropriate).
- Shorten.
- Teach format ahead of time.

## Communicating to the Student

- Avoid using terms like *later* and *maybe* and sarcasm.
- Be concrete and specific.
- If necessary, break tasks into smaller steps.
- Provide information about expectations.
- Provide warnings about change.

- Slow down the pace, allowing student time to process information (three–six seconds).
- Use gestures, modeling, and demonstrations with verbalizations.

### Encouraging Communication With the Student

- Encourage input and choice when possible.
- Model correct format without corrections.
- Pause, listen, and wait.
- Respond positively to attempts.
- Watch and listen to attempts to respond.

### Social Supports

- Create cooperative learning situations where student may share proficiencies.
- Develop social stories.
- Establish a buddy system.
- Focus on social process rather than end product.
- Practice specific skills through natural activities with one or more peers.
- Praise classmates when they treat students properly; discourage teasing.
- Structure activities with set interaction patterns and roles (when appropriate).
- Teach, rehearse, practice, model, and reinforce the following skills: turn taking, responding, waiting, greeting, joining others, taking the lead, joking and teasing, and complimenting.

### Environment and Routine

- Allow modifications to accommodate sensory problems when necessary.
- Avoid surprises by preparing student in advance.
- Minimize transitions.
- Offer a consistent daily routine.
- Provide a predictable and safe environment.
- Recognize distractions and sources of sensory overload (e.g., hearing, vision, smell, tactile).

### Self-Management/Behavior

- Avoid disciplinary actions for behaviors that may be part of the child's disability.

- Avoid punitive measures; use positive and natural consequences.
- Determine why behavior is occurring and develop behavior plan.
- Encourage choices when appropriate.
- Incorporate strengths and interests into daily activities.
- Provide reinforcement that is individualized, immediate, and concrete.
- Teach use of visual schedule, cues, and timer.

## Strategies for Adapting Tests and Quizzes

### Preparing for Tests and Quizzes

- Provide review time during or outside of class, emphasizing key points to study.
- Provide students with examples of test content and format.
- Provide study guides in advance of the test.
- Teach strategies to prepare for a test or quiz.
- Teach what to look for in test questions—how to "read" a test.
- Use a variety of formats to review thoroughly for several days before tests or quizzes, including quiz bowls, small-group review, question and answer periods, and study buddies.

### Writing Tests or Quizzes

- Avoid penalizing for grammar, handwriting, or spelling.
- Give more objective than subjective items.
- Give shorter tests, covering less information, more frequently.
- Increase allowable time for test completion.
- Reduce the test items by starring those that assess the most important concepts. Give the same test to all students but score some students on the priority items only, giving extra credit for any additional questions answered correctly.
- Review orally to ensure comprehension of essay questions.
- Underline or highlight important words in the test directions or on test items.
- Vary the test format (e.g., written, oral, short answer, essay, multiple-choice, matching, yes/no, demonstration testing, open book/notes, take-home, cooperative group testing).
- Write clear, concise directions.

### Administering and Scoring Tests and Quizzes

- Allow students to grade their own tests immediately upon completion in a designated area; the teacher does the final scoring.

- Allow students to retake the test and give credit for improvement.
- Allow students to take the test in small groups; students may use a group answer or their own.
- Allow students to take the test in the classroom during the scheduled time and give opportunities to have it read to them orally; average the two scores.
- Allow students to tape-record answers.
- Allow students to use charts, calculators, or manipulatives that they have used on assignments for the exam.
- Correct tests immediately and reteach in skill groups.
- Create a modified grading scale or consider a pass/fail or satisfactory/unsatisfactory grade on the test.
- Encourage students to chart their progress.
- Give students opportunities to critique their own work based on your criteria before they hand it in.
- Grade student effort and individual ability in addition to test scores.
- Provide feedback to students via teacher-student conferences.
- Provide partial credit for correct steps in a problem-solving process.
- Provide students with the opportunity to have tests read orally.
- Read test instructions aloud to any student who would prefer them read aloud.
- Take time to review corrected tests and allow students to make corrections on their test or a clean copy of the test.
- Tape-record tests, using assistants, tutors, parent volunteers, and others.

### Providing Alternatives to Tests and Quizzes

- Provide a menu of options for students to demonstrate knowledge other than or in addition to tests:
  - Allow students to design their own project/demonstrations.
  - Conduct interviews of individuals who have something to say about the unit of study.
  - Create maps, graphs, diagrams.
  - Design and play simulation game activities.
  - Design collages, posters, time lines of events, story boards.
  - Develop and conduct a survey.
  - Find a guest speaker.
  - Keep a journal.
  - Participate in discussions.

o Point to a picture cue system for test/quiz responses.
o Provide a packet of activities that students complete throughout the unit.
o Write and perform skits.
- Provide information on the standard report card indicating the adaptations that have been made.
- Vary the grading system; grade on items other than the tests (e.g., homework, special projects).
- Offer extra-credit activities throughout the grading period.
- Use a grading contract, detailing the basis for grades.
- In secondary programs, consider an audit system to allow students to take classes that provide knowledge but do not result in a credit or grade.
- Allow test partners
  o Offer using test partners as a student option.
  o Each student has his or her own set of notes and copy of the test.
  o Student partners are allowed to read and discuss questions; then each student writes his or her own answer.
  o Students each have their own test so that if there is disagreement, they can write their own answer.
  o Both partners must be present on the day of the test, or the test is taken alone.

## Adapting Response Mode

A child can exhibit knowledge in numerous ways. A very important option when working with children with special needs is to offer options that take into account learning style, modality strengths (e.g., visual learner), age, developmental motor skills, and attention span. Another very important factor in adapting the curriculum is to consider the use of a variety of response modes for the child with a learning disability. Providing many different options will increase the likelihood of success. Some options for changing response mode include the following:

| | |
|---|---|
| animated movie | game board |
| commentary | poster |
| book | speech |
| display | mobile |
| scavenger hunt | tape |

| | |
|---|---|
| panel discussion | tour |
| interview | charades |
| portrait | television show |
| pantomime | invention |
| play | radio |
| model | radio commercial |
| skit | puppet show |
| song | slide presentation |
| report | bulletin board |
| poem | cookbook |
| puzzle | telephone talk |
| map | maze |
| cartoon | show case |
| magazine | banner |
| comic strip | visual art form |
| diorama | script |
| brochure | brainteasers |
| collage | diary |
| newspaper | time capsule |
| blueprint | videotape recording |
| survey | mural |
| sculpture | time line |

In conclusion, there are numerous ways to present, record, and ask children to respond to curriculum material. Our job as educators is to ensure that we have done everything possible to help children succeed and gain a sense of accomplishment in school. Since there are so many options in adapting the curriculum available to us, it is crucial that we explore and try these options. You never know what will work.

# Step VI

# Classroom Management of Children With Specific Disabilities

The individuality of students' needs should be a primary concern for any teacher. However, the type of disability will play an important part in determining the strategies that you will use to help the students adjust and perform to their abilities. As a special education teacher, you will be required to adapt the curriculum and make necessary modifications to increase the student's chances of success.

If you are working in a regular education setting, you will come into contact with high-incidence disabilities. These may include the following:

- Learning disabilities
- Mental retardation: Note that the label of *mental retardation (MR)*, while used in IDEA, may vary from state to state. For instance, some states use *cognitively delayed* or *cognitive disability (CD)* in place of MR.
- Emotional disabilities
- Attention deficit/hyperactivity disorder (ADHD)

This section will deal with the curriculum adaptations for these specific disabilities.

# Students With Learning Disabilities

Working with students with learning disabilities can be a challenge, since there are numerous types of learning disabilities (e.g., dyslexia, dyscalculia, visual-motor impairments). As a result, the teacher should be aware that not all techniques will work with all students but try as many of them as possible. The goal of any adaptation is to increase the student's chances of understanding the material and increase the chances of completion and success.

## Adjust the Means of Presentation and Evaluation

Since students with learning disabilities have different strengths and weaknesses, methods of presentation (e.g., visual, auditory) must be considered. If you have done your homework, then you will be aware of the learning styles of each student and the ways in which each child will learn best. Some students learn better by seeing (visual learners), some by listening (auditory learners), some by feeling (tactile learners), and some by a combination of approaches. The teacher should make adjustments to determine the best functional system of learning for the children with learning disabilities. This will vary from child to child and is usually included in the child's evaluation.

If the student learns best through material that is presented through the auditory channel, then you may want to consider the following examples:

- Give verbal as well as written directions to assignments.
- Have students close their eyes to focus on hearing words or information.
- Have students drill aloud to themselves or to other students.
- Place assignment directions on tape so that students can replay them when they need to.
- Give students oral rather than written tests. In this way, you will be able to judge better the student's level of knowledge without a perceptual weakness clouding the results.
- Make adjustments to the type of assignment, the level of difficulty, and amount and sequence of material presented to students with learning disabilities.
- It is strongly suggested that you correct and hand back each student's work as soon as possible to allow for immediate gratification and feedback. This will also increase the motivation for the next assignment.

- Shorten the length of the assignments to ensure a sense of success. In this way, the students will be able to accomplish more and feel good about themselves.
- Make copies of chapters of textbooks so that the student can use a highlighter pen to underline important facts. Using a multisensory approach will enhance the chances of the student's remembering what is being read. Reading aloud, highlighting, making notes on the page, and seeing the material will utilize a variety of senses.
- Make sure that the child's desk is free from all unnecessary materials. A common factor in the lives of many students with learning disabilities is disorganization. Clutter and trouble organizing materials is common and can interfere in learning.
- Make adjustments to the work space and amount of time given for assignment.
- Try to alternate quiet and active time to maintain levels of interest and motivation.
- Develop a work contract with specific times and assignments so that the child has a structured idea of his responsibilities.
- Depending on how you design your classroom, you may want the student to work in a quiet corner or use a study carrel. This technique depends on the specific learning style of the child, who may be less distracted by working under these conditions.
- Place the student closer to you to receive more immediate feedback. In this way, you will also be able to see the work style and attention to task and determine whether proximity to the teacher has a positive effect on the student's ability to accomplish work.
- Try to separate the student from others who may be distracting. Since distraction is a common symptom, you will need to evaluate your population and make seating arrangements that facilitate learning.

If the child is primarily a visual learner, consider the following examples when adjusting the mode of presentation:

- Encourage students to write down notes to themselves concerning important words, concepts, and ideas.
- Offer the student an outline of the material that will be presented if you are going to lecture. In this way he or she will have a visual outline and be able to follow the lesson better.
- Have students use flash cards printed in bold bright colors.
- Let students close their eyes and try to visualize words or information in their heads (i.e., to see things in their minds).

# Students With Mental Retardation

What is a mental disability?

A student can be defined as having a mental disability if certain learning, social, and behavior patterns are exhibited to a marked extent and over a prolonged period of time. Such patterns may include the following:

- Consistently slow rate of learning such that the child's level of development resembles that of a younger child
- Delays in most areas of development
- A consistently subaverage intellectual level
- Impaired adaptive functioning in such areas as social skills, communication, and daily living skills

Some common characteristics of a mild mental disability that may be observed by the teacher over a period of time include the following:

- Difficulty getting started
- Difficulty with abstract concepts
- Resistance to change
- Short attention span
- Difficulty with abstract concepts
- Difficulty generalizing learned concepts to new situations
- Social isolation or withdrawal
- Anxious and worried, having excessive fears and phobias
- Easily frustrated even when confronted with a simple task

Students with mild mental retardation learn in the same way as normal students. However, adaptations and a variety of techniques need to be utilized. Consequently, certain behaviors should be targeted as priorities when dealing with mentally disabled children in the classroom. These target areas include the following:

- General work habits
- Functional academic skills
- Vocational and career awareness

## Techniques for Teaching
## Children With Mental Retardation

Following are some examples of techniques that may help the child attain functional academics.

*General*

- Provide students with activities that will reinforce independent work. If the activity is too hard, the student may become too dependent on teacher supervision.
- Employ practice activities for any basic skill that may relate to the student's daily life problems.
- Have materials that are commensurate with the student's skill levels.

*Reading*

- Have the student collect food labels and compare the differences.
- Allow the student to look up the names of the student's family members in the phone book. Use the smaller local guide for this activity.
- Have activities that focus on reading for information and leisure.
- Activities that require the student to become more aware of the surrounding environment, such as having the child list the names of all food stores in the community, all hospitals, and so on, will increase familiarity with the environment.

*Math*

- Provide the opportunity for the student make up a budget for using his or her allowance.
- Encourage the student to cook in school or at home to become more familiar with measurements.
- Have the student record the daily temperature.
- Involve the student in measuring the height of classmates.
- Allow student to buy something at the school store or take part in running the store. The student could help by sorting pencils, arranging supplies, counting the number of items left (helping with inventory), and sorting the money that was collected.
- Students could collect lunch envelopes or attendance folders from classrooms in the morning. These skills can help with room/number identification.

*Handwriting/Spelling*

- Encourage the student to make a list of things to do for the day.
- Have the student run a messenger service in the classroom so that the student can write the messages and deliver them from one student to another.

Examples of helping the child improve general work habits may include the following:

### Completing Work Assignments

- Evaluate the length and level of an assignment to make sure it is within the ability level of the child.
- Provide shorter but more frequent assignments.
- Assign reward activities that are contingent upon successful completion of work.
- Encourage the student to maintain a performance chart on the number of tasks completed each day.

### Attendance at School

- Assist the student in maintaining a record of attendance and on-time behavior.
- Create a make-believe time clock that the child has to punch in on when entering the classroom.
- Emphasize to the student the importance of being on time to class.
- Do not be afraid to express your expectations in clear terms concerning attendance and punctuality.

### Working With Peers

- Collaborate with the school psychologist and see if that professional can run a group in your classroom.
- Offer the student a simple job that requires the other students to go to him or her. For example, place the student in charge of attendance and check off the other children when they report in.
- Encourage the child to start a hobby and then start a hobby club involving other students.
- Allow the student to be part of a team that takes care of the class pets or some other class activity. Calling it a "team" will make the child feel more connected.

## Vocational and Career Skill Development

Career awareness is a skill that can be part of the classroom curriculum in many ways. Many of the skills mentioned above will enhance the child's career skills, which should focus on adapting to and integrating into society.

# Students With Emotional Disabilities

Adapting the curriculum for students with emotional disabilities may not meet the real needs of these students. The issues that need to be addressed more than likely will involve management concerns, which can be found later in this section. If you need to adapt the curriculum, use any of the suggestions found in other disability areas as well as those below.

## Helping the Student Complete Classwork Assignments

- Help the student become organized by keeping very little in his desk and by using a bound book for writing rather than a loose-leaf binder where pages can fall out and add to disorganization. Also supply large folders for the child to keep work in and so on.
- Be very specific on what you mean by *neat, organized,* and so on. Abstract labels have different meanings to different people. Say, "Please be neat, and by *neat* I mean. . . ."
- Develop a contract with the child where the student can determine the rewards for completion.
- Finds ways to compensate (e.g., word processor) if the student's handwriting is beyond correction.

# Students With Attention Deficit/Hyperactivity Disorder

Classroom teachers of students with ADHD can adjust certain factors to accommodate the individual curriculum needs of these children. Some examples include the following:

## Organization

- Students with organizational problems will usually maintain very disorganized notes, notebooks, desks, and lockers. Give the students a weekly task of organizing these areas. Making this task part of the contract and routine will also make the students feel better about themselves.
- Make a copy of homework assignments and hand it to the student at the end of the day. This will alleviate a great deal of stress for the student, especially if the student is disorganized and frequently forgets to copy the homework.

- Work with the parent in developing a program to organize the student at night. Have the parent develop a checklist so that the student's clothes, books, assignments, and so on are ready for the next morning. The stress and disorganization of the morning should be reduced if at all possible. This will result in a more pleasant experience at home and help the student feel more secure when going to school.
- Try to avoid giving multiple directions or multiple assignments whenever possible. Allow the student to finish one assignment or direction at a time before going on to the next.

## Academic Skills

- Window out single math problems so that the student only sees one at a time. This can be accomplished by cutting out a square on a piece of paper that the student can move from one problem to the next, covering all the other problems.
- For older students, allow them to have a sheet with the formulas already printed. Asking them to memorize may reduce their ability to accomplish the task. The less they have to worry about, the more they may be able to finish.
- Determine what your goal is when presenting an assignment. Once you have done this, pave all the roads for the student up to that point. For example, if your goal is to see if the student can find the circumference of a circle, provide her with the necessary formulas, definitions, and examples. These materials will reduce frustration and confusion and increase chances of success.
- Have the student do five problems, two questions, and so on at a time. Then have the student come up for immediate feedback. Numerous successful tasks can only add to confidence levels. This will also prevent the student from progressing too far while making the same error.
- Allow the student to use graph paper while doing math. In this way, the student will have a structured environment in which to place numbers. Use very large graph paper so that the student has little difficulty placing one number in each box. This will keep him organized and focused.
- Do not use bubble sheets. Allow the student to answer directly in the booklet or on the paper. Reducing the amount of movement during academic tasks is beneficial since ADHD students have difficulty refocusing.

# Step VII

# Apply Instructional Interventions for Specific Behaviors Exhibited in the Classroom by Students With Emotional and/or Behavioral Disorders

## Instructional Interventions for Active Noncompliance

### Examples of Behavior

- Actively refuses to follow directions (e.g., "no" or "I won't").
- Acts bored (e.g., "This is dumb" or rolls eyes).

- Assignments not finished.
- Makes comments or walks away, even leaves room.
- Poor work quality (e.g., messy, carelessly done).
- Spends lots of time looking for work or materials.
- Stalls or dawdles.

## Desired Alternative Behavior(s)

- Asks for clarification if doesn't understand the task (e.g., by raising hand, waiting for teacher to finish speaking).
- Begins work within ___ minutes (or seconds) (e.g., gets materials out, opens books, begins task).
- Completes work neatly (e.g., handwriting is legible, paper is not wrinkled or smudged).
- Follows directions within ___ minutes (or seconds) without arguing or talking back.
- Shows good effort by having materials ready, beginning task within ___ minutes/seconds, attempting difficult tasks.
- Waits for turn to speak by raising hand, waiting for teacher acknowledgment.

## General Instructional Strategies That Might Be Useful in Teaching the Desired Behavior(s)

- Ask yourself what the bottom line issue is. For example, if it's getting the assignment done, then perhaps reinforce getting it done and work on neatness as the next step.
- Be gentle when cueing, correcting, redirecting, etc. The goal is to connect with, not push, the student further away.
- Break multistep activities into smaller steps, providing feedback and reinforcement along the way. Break long-term assignments into smaller, short-term tasks.
- Have clear expectations, allow student input, and review them periodically.
- Offer choices in tasks and assignments, allowing the student to focus on his or her strengths and interests.
- Seat the student near the teacher, away from distractions, etc.
- Teach expectations and classroom procedures.
- Teach organizational skills and time management.
- Teach students problem-solving skills and decision-making skills.

# Instructional Interventions for Attendance Problems

## Examples of Behavior

- Gets far behind in schoolwork and gives up, cannot participate in ongoing class activities, and/or cannot reasonably catch up.
- Misses the whole class or day.
- Has poor or inconsistent attendance, even if excused.
- Is regularly late for class.
- Skips class but doesn't leave the school campus.

## Desired Alternative Behavior(s)

- Attends school regularly (each class, entire day).
- Is on time to class (define: in seat when bell rings? In room when bell rings?).
- Completes makeup work.
- Is on time for class and ready to work (has necessary materials).

## General Instructional Strategies That Might Be Useful in Teaching the Desired Behavior(s)

- Enact a short-term intervention where the student's attendance is checked daily for some period of time (two or three weeks) and attendance is reinforced and rewarded. After that period, look at whether attendance has improved (so perhaps you can back off and only check weekly or every three or four days), stayed the same (maybe try it another week), or not improved and perhaps gotten worse (in which case it may be "back to the drawing board").
- Anticipate lateness: seat the student near the door and have work on the desk and ready if/when the student arrives.
- Consider whether the school wants to have a consistent definition of *on time* so that it is the same for all.
- Contract for work based on amount of work to be completed rather than time limits.
- Depending on the underlying issues, refer the student to the guidance counselor, school social worker, or school psychologist. Also, could any community agencies be of help?
- Double up (spend more time on fewer subject areas) so that student can salvage something for the grading period.

- Have a plan for the student to make up the work (doing independent study, demonstrating mastery rather than turning in every assignment, etc.). Keep from overwhelming the student.
- Have a task to be done as soon as students enter the room—it gives you time to set up, take attendance, and do other housekeeping chores but keeps them busy. The task can be a review of yesterday's lesson, a lead-in for today, journaling, creative writing, current events, etc.
- Involve the school nurse to make sure the student has no serious health issues.
- Make sure the student knows what *on time* means, and make sure student knows this for all classes.
- Provide a program that is motivating and reinforcing to the student, especially initially. Start with classes in which the student has skill or enjoys and build from there.
- Provide an alarm clock or give a wake-up call to the student.
- Reinforce progress, not just perfection.
- Reinforce the desired behavior.
- The school may not be able to do this alone. Could other agencies, programs, or individuals be involved?
- Implement service learning. Note that while the activity may be fun for the student (and not a "punishment" or negative consequence), the goal is to connect the student with the schools and/or peers. Punishment makes the least sense in these instances.
- Implement truancy abatement programs, such as providing a "neutral site" program where students can catch up with work, deal with issues, and have some support for returning to school. Some communities have worked with the Boys/Girls Club to establish such programs, and they are often cooperative efforts among the school district, social services, and the club. Students may be brought to the site by the police or parents rather than being returned to the school building.
- Try to "prime" success for the students when they return to school or attend. Make sure the first tasks are motivating and successful for them so that they feel competent and motivated to continue to attend.
- Use homework for bonus point for all kids.
- Work with the student to find afterschool or partial-day employment if money is an issue; find ways for student to "earn" needed or desired items.

# Instructional Interventions for Difficulty With Transitions

## Examples of Behavior

- Actively resists activity change by having a tantrum, pushing, shoving, acting out, or verbal aggression.
- Has difficulty moving from one place or activity to another.
- Has difficulty starting and/or stopping an activity.
- Has difficulty with changes of routine (e.g., substitute teacher, fire drills, assemblies, shortened days due to weather or inservice times).
- Refuses to stop an activity, especially after being directed to do so.

## Desired Alternative Behavior(s)

- Demonstrates organizational skills (e.g., prioritizes tasks, can leave tasks unfinished and return later to complete them).
- Follows teacher directions regarding the schedule and changes of activities.
- Keeps hands and feet to self (e.g., remains at least an arm's or leg's length away from others) when moving to another area or standing in line.
- Shifts from one activity to the next within ___ (amount of time).
- Uses appropriate conversation skills during unstructured times and transitions (e.g., acceptable tone and language with no swearing or shouting, acceptable volume for indoor settings).

## General Instructional Strategies That Might Be Useful in Teaching the Desired Behavior(s)

- Actively engage students in learning activities to increase on-task behavior.
- Adjust demands depending on the time (e.g., student is on medications and it is almost time for another dose, just before lunch, end of the day).
- Allow time for the student to process the request and respond.
- Use cooperative learning.
- Use direct instruction.
- Foreshadow (e.g., "Three more minutes to finish up.").
- If transitioning from a favorite to a less-favorite activity, prime the student for compliance by giving a task that will probably

be complied with, then move to the next activity. For example, say, "Billy, bring me a dictionary, please," because the dictionary is close to Billy and he will probably bring it to you. Then say, "Thank you—now please sit at the large table." You can also reinforce Billy for complying with your request, which might ease him into the next task.

- Use modeling.
- Use a peer mentoring/buddy system.
- Post a daily schedule, making sure also to post changes.
- Implement a response cost/token economy.
- Use role-playing.
- Use self-monitoring/checking.
- Use sensory integration techniques (the student may be over- or understimulated).
- Use social stories and comic book conversations.
- Use learning centers.
- Vary instructional presentations.

## Instructional Interventions for Disrespect to Teachers

### Examples of Behavior

- Deliberately pushes the limits, openly defying the teacher.
- Draws inappropriate pictures, such as caricatures.
- Mimics, makes faces, uses inappropriate gestures such as "the finger."
- Engages in name-calling or swearing.
- Is rude, talks back, or interrupts.
- Has "selective hearing," ignoring the teacher.
- Uses creative writing assignments to disrespect teachers.
- Walks away while the teacher is talking.
- Writes inappropriate messages on notebooks or folders.

### Desired Alternative Behavior(s)

- Asks to take a break or self-timeout, using a prearranged phrase or nonverbal cue.
- Develops a script or cues to use and role-plays those alternatives.
- Disagrees respectfully (e.g., by using a preapproved script and by speaking in a conversational tone).

- Postpones discussion until time allows and student and teacher have had a chance to think.
- Talks or vents through journaling, writing, or drawing within previously determined guidelines (e.g., appropriate language, no threats).
- Uses active listening.

## General Instructional Strategies That Might Be Useful in Teaching the Desired Behavior(s)

- Brainstorm and discuss real-life consequences of verbal and nonverbal disrespect.
- Give the students time to think about how they want to fix the problem (apologize face-to-face, write a letter, make a card, make restitution).
- Involve the student in school counseling groups that focus on various topics (alcohol and other drug abuse [AODA], divorce, anger management, grief, stress relief, self-esteem).
- Use peer mediation
- Use scripting: role-play inappropriate behaviors and write better responses.
- Teach and model active listening.
- Teach anger management.
- Teach conflict resolution skills.
- Teach empathy and perspective taking.
- Teach stress-relief strategies.
- Use *I* messages.
- Use video clips or vignettes as a basis for discussion (helps to relieve defensiveness).

# Instructional Interventions for Classroom Disruption

## Examples of Behavior

- Bothers other students, trying to engage them in conversation.
- Gets out of seat and wanders around the room.
- Makes inappropriate noises (tapping pencil, humming, animal noises, play noises such as imitating airplanes or motorcycles, etc.).
- Laughs/giggles at inappropriate times.
- Throws things.
- Tries to engage other students in conversation.

### Desired Alternative Behavior(s)

- Asks to move; asks for a break.
- Indicates unable to do work.
- Raises hand or uses other teacher-approved cue (e.g., eye contact, writing on slate, holding up card) to answer during class time.
- Remains in seat for ____ minutes (or during instructional activity) unless given teacher permission to get up.
- Remains on-task (e.g., writing, reading, drawing) for a minimum of _____ minutes.
- Seeks help with a problem.
- Tells what *on-task* or *topic-related* means.
- Uses acceptable tone and volume of voice.
- Uses movement options/breaks without bothering other students or making noise.

### General Instructional Strategies That Might Be Useful in Teaching the Desired Behavior(s)

- Adjust demands at critical times (e.g., just before lunch; end of the day; just before student needs medication; after an especially hard, stressful task).
- Develop classroom rules as a group.
- Use erasable, individual slates or another type of board so the student writes down the question or answer he or she just has to say right now. Can then show it to the teacher with little or no calling out or classroom disruption.
- Give choices within classroom versus teacher-directed activities only.
- Provide physical breaks, sensory breaks, and movement options.
- Provide instruction on what to do when, turn taking, how to "signal," what cues to look for, reading social situations and cues.
- Teach empathy and perspective taking.
- Teach errors in thinking.
- Teach social skills and provide opportunities to practice them.
- Give teacher- or student-assigned "jobs" in cooperative groups, giving everyone responsibility and encouraging students to follow group expectations.
- Provide verbal cues for student to use to self-cue as reminders of what she is supposed to be doing (e.g., "At this moment, am I . . . ?").

# Instructional Interventions for Failure to Accept Responsibility for Own Behavior and/or Consequences for Misbehavior

## Examples of Behavior

- Argues when confronted with a situation.
- Argues/resists consequences.
- Does not admit to wrongdoing.
- Does not take ownership of conflicts.

## Desired Alternative Behavior(s)

- Accepts consequences without arguing or whining.
- Talks through the incident with a teacher or counselor and identifies alternatives for behavior (admitting responsibility, apologizing, restitution).
- Tells how the behavior affects others.
- When presented with a problem situation, admits a mistake was made.
- When presented with wrongdoing, tells the truth regarding participation.

## General Instructional Strategies That Might Be Useful in Teaching the Desired Behavior(s)

- Use behavioral contracting.
- Teach errors in thinking.
- Use organized activities during recess.
- Use overcorrection (requiring the student to perform the appropriate behavior repeatedly in the environment/situation where the misbehavior occurred and repeatedly reinforcing the student for exhibiting the appropriate behavior).
- Teach perspective taking and empathy.
- Implement restorative justice.
- Use role-playing.
- Use scripting.
- Use service learning.
- Use social stories.
- Teach a skill to the entire class, then use peers for reinforcement and modeling; use group contingencies or reinforcement.

# Instructional Interventions for Interpersonal Relationships With Peers

## Examples of Behavior

- Has difficulty interacting with peers (joining a group, playing a game, initiating and continuing social conversations, taking turns, etc.).
- Interrupts conversations.
- Refuses to share and/or take turns.
- Is rude/impolite.
- Tattles.

## Desired Alternative Behavior(s)

- Uses effective social skills in various school settings (e.g., hall, lunchroom, study hall, all classrooms).
- Takes turns while playing a game in informal settings.
- Independently shares toys/materials during group activities.
- Listens quietly while others talk and waits his or her turn to speak.
- Uses pretaught steps in determining when to tell the teacher versus when to let it go untold (e.g., telling if there is a safety issue).

## General Instructional Strategies That Might Be Useful in Teaching the Desired Behavior(s)

- Use behavior contracting.
- Hold class meetings.
- Don't punish other students solely on the basis of tattling.
- Correct gently if behaviors are occasional or if reported behavior is not serious.
- Model acceptable behavior (teacher and peers).
- Use precorrection/prompts.
- Use role-playing.
- Provide supervised play and structured activities during recess or other free time.
- Teach manners and politeness.
- Teach the difference between unnecessary tattling and reporting serious behavior.

# Instructional Interventions for Out-of-Control Behaviors

## Examples of Behavior

- Is a danger to self and/or others.
- Is unable to calm down/regroup and continue after an outburst.
- Engages in self-injurious behavior or self-mutilation, such as scratching self, burning self with cigarette, etc.
- Throws tantrums.

## Desired Alternative Behavior(s)

- Identifies appropriate ways to behave in crisis/conflict.
- Problem-solves appropriate ways to regain control.
- Refrains from hurting self.
- Remains calm when faced with difficult situations.

## General Instructional Strategies That Might Be Useful in Teaching the Desired Behavior(s)

- Ask, "What triggered the problem? How can I get the student back into being successful?"
- Use bibliotherapy.
- Use direct teaching of social skills.
- Discuss real-life consequences of verbal and nonverbal behaviors.
- Teach relaxation or stress-reduction techniques.
- Use role-playing or modeling.
- Use social stories.
- Teach alternative activities to deal with built-up or escalating emotional tension.
- Teach anger management skills.
- Teach negotiation skills, conflict resolution strategies, problem-solving skills.

# Instructional Interventions for Passive Resistance

## Examples of Behavior

- "Just sits."
- Appears depressed (sad, flat affect, lethargic).

- Is disengaged.
- Refuses to work (passive, not disruptive).
- Sleeps in class.
- Is withdrawn.

## Desired Alternative Behavior(s)

- Actively participates in classroom activities (e.g., stays awake, asks questions, talks when appropriate, participates in small-group activities).
- Completes assignments (with a minimum of ____ percent accuracy, on time, turned in).
- Remains on task (e.g., reading or writing, working on assignment) for ____ minutes.
- Resumes task within ____ seconds/minutes with no more than one prompt.
- Uses attentive body language (e.g., head up, eye contact, following along).

## General Instructional Strategies That Might Be Useful in Teaching the Desired Behavior(s)

- Encourage catching up. Use buddy system, give the students a "snapshot" of the day/activity/lesson missed, call the students at home to say you missed them, welcome them back.
- Give choices (on homework, alternative testing options).
- Give extra credit (one point) for a pertinent question asked.
- Give students responsibility you know they will want and that will be motivating.
- Have students develop materials for other students (cross-age or same-age).
- Have the students help in a classroom where they have been successful in the past.
- Teach organization skills in each class, in homeroom, or in study hall by using differently colored folders for each class, assignment notebooks, etc.
- Allow passive breaks to provide time to relax, put head down, nap (if health or sleep deprivation is an issue).
- Plug into the students' strengths; start small and build on success.
- Teach social skills. Use small groups, cooperative learning, lab partners, cross-age tutoring, literature circles (each member has a role such as leader, recorder, vocabulary, etc., and members rotate roles).

- For students who are reluctant to ask questions or speak out, have them write questions on a piece of paper and then give them a written response. Be sure to compliment the student (e.g., "Good question," or "Would you ask that question tomorrow in the large group?"). You might also send another student with the same question to the target student for an answer.

# Instructional Interventions for Not Respecting Property or Personal Space of Others

## Examples of Behavior

- Damages an item that is not the student's own.
- Fails to return an item loaned.
- Invades another's personal space; gets too close.
- Takes things from others without permission.

## Desired Alternative Behavior(s)

- Asks permission to use an item.
- Maintains a reasonable distance from others; respects their personal space.
- Returns borrowed item after use in reasonable or agreed-upon time.
- Returns borrowed item undamaged.

## General Instructional Strategies That Might Be Useful in Teaching the Desired Behavior(s)

- Have a "glove tree" to make certain students have some winter clothing, etc.
- Develop activities to develop/improve self-esteem.
- Use behavior contracting.
- Create and reinforce activities in which students work together for a common goal.
- Establish rules for sharing school materials, bringing personal belongings to school/class (toys, portable electronics, etc.).
- Have a supply of school materials so that students have the materials they need.
- Implement restorative justice if items are damaged.
- Give tangible rewards and/or social praise for sharing.
- Teach social skills.

- Use cooperative learning.
- Use smaller groups.

# Instructional Interventions for Verbal Aggression

## Examples of Behavior

- Harasses others; uses racial slurs.
- Engages in name-calling or put-downs.
- Uses obscene or profane language.
- Screams, yells, makes loud remarks.
- Makes sexual comments or gang comments.
- Makes threats or bullies others.

## Desired Alternative Behavior(s)

- Demonstrates respect to others in language used, tone of voice, and voice volume.
- Refrains from name-calling, making threats, bullying, making gang comments, making sexual comments, and using obscene language.
- Requests adult assistance to deal with conflict.
- Tells why certain language/comments are not acceptable and chooses acceptable alternatives.
- Uses acceptable language to give compliments and in social conversations (give examples of words or phrases student should use).
- Uses conflict resolution/problem-solving strategies when in a conflict situation (identifies problem, lists options, identifies consequences, chooses one, evaluates effectiveness of choice, reviews/revises).
- Uses socially acceptable and respectful language.
- Walks away from conflict/escalating situation.

## General Instructional Strategies That Might Be Useful in Teaching the Desired Behavior(s)

- Build self-esteem so student won't feel a need to denigrate others.
- Communicate with parents about concerns to find out what they allow or don't allow with their child.
- Does the student know why comments are unacceptable? There may be cultural/ethnic issues. If so, talk to student and explain the problem. Teach alternatives.

- Intervene early when student begins to make inappropriate comments to others so situation does not escalate.
- Model appropriate language at all times.
- Use peer mediation.
- Script and role-play better responses and appropriate language.
- Use small-group counseling (empathy, acceptance of differences, respect, etc.).
- Teach anger management and stress relief.
- Set expectations of an emotionally safe environment for all students.

# Instructional Interventions for Verbal Outbursts

## Examples of Behavior

- Argues with peers and/or adults.
- Calls out.
- Makes disruptive noises (humming, animal sounds, etc.).
- Screams or yells.
- Talks out.

## Desired Alternative Behavior(s)

- Accepts criticism without arguing.
- Asks for adult assistance to deal with teasing or other conflict.
- Develops a script or cues to use and role-play/practice.
- Disagrees appropriately (e.g., using preselected statements).
- Discusses issue with adult or peer without becoming defensive.
- Follows classroom rules while participating in classroom activities.
- Ignores peers rather than teasing them.
- Lists ways in which his behavior affects others.
- Raises hand.
- Sits quietly during quiet times.
- Walks away from conflict.

## General Instructional Strategies That Might Be Useful in Teaching the Desired Behavior(s)

- Allow movement breaks, sensory options, or physical breaks.
- Give the student time to process and problem-solve.
- Use role-playing.
- Teach social skills.

- Use social stories.
- Teach and model desired behaviors.
- Teach anger management strategies.
- Teach conflict resolution strategies.
- Teach stress relief.
- Use a token economy system.

# Step VIII

# Understanding Grading Options for Students With Special Needs

W hen working with children with special needs, one of the most difficult decisions for teachers is how to grade students. This process presents a dilemma for all educators. If we use traditional competitive grading systems, then students who try, participate, and finish assignments but because of their disability fail tests will receive a failing grade when compared to their peers.

## Grading Options

This type of approach may lead to frustration, loss of motivation, parent frustration, and a "why bother attitude" on the part of the child. On the other hand, grading students solely on attitude, effort, accountability, responsibility, etc., despite failing grades, may mislead both parents and students into setting unrealistic goals.

Salend (2001) describes a variety of student grading systems that you may want to consider when determining your students' grades.

*Numeric/letter grades:* Teachers assign numeric or letter grades based on students' performance on tests or specific learning activities.

*Checklists/rating scales:* Teachers develop checklists and rating scales that delineate the benchmarks associated with their courses and evaluate each student according to mastery of these benchmarks. Some school districts have revised their grading systems by creating rating scales for different grade levels. Teachers rate students on each skill, using a scale that includes "not yet evident," "beginning," "developing," and "independent."

*Anecdotal/descriptive and portfolio grading:* Teachers write descriptive comments regarding students' skills, learning styles, effort, attitudes, and growth and write strategies to improve student performance. These comments can be included with examples of students' work as part of portfolio grading.

*Pass/fail systems:* Minimum course competencies are specified, and students who demonstrate mastery receive a P grade, while those who fail to meet the minimum standards are given an F. Some schools have modified the traditional pass/fail grading system to include such distinctions as honors (Honor-P), high pass (HP), pass (P), and low pass (LP).

*Mastery level/criterion systems:* Students and teachers meet to divide the material into a hierarchy of skills and activities based on an assessment of individual needs and abilities. After completing the learning activities, students take a posttest or perform an activity to demonstrate mastery of the content. When students demonstrate mastery, they receive credit for that accomplishment and repeat the process with the next skill to be mastered.

*Progressive improvement grading:* Students take exams and engage in learning activities and receive feedback and instruction based on their performance throughout the grading period. Only performance on cumulative tests and learning activities during the final weeks of the grading period, however, is used to determine students' grades.

*Multiple grading:* Teachers grade students in the areas of ability, effort, and achievement. Students' report cards can include a listing of the three grades for each content area, or grades can be computed by weighting the three areas.

*Level grading:* Teachers use a numeric subscript to indicate the level of difficulty on which the students' grades are based. For example, a grade of $B_6$ can be used to note that a student is working in the B range at the sixth-grade level. Subscript systems can also be devised to indicate whether students are working at grade level, above grade level, or below grade level.

*Contract grading:* Teachers and students agree on a contract outlining the learning objectives; the amount, nature, and quality of the products students must complete; and the procedures for evaluating student products and assigning a grade.

*Individualized Education Program (IEP) Grading:* Teachers assign grades that acknowledge students' progress in meeting IEP goals and performance criteria.

## Reporting to Parents

What you will find as a teacher of children with special needs is that the parents receive a great deal of reassurance from any information coming from the school concerning the child's progress. Keeping parents in the dark only results in anxiety and negative assumptions. Do not be afraid to communicate progress to parents as often as possible. Parents place a higher priority on receiving information about their children's progress than any other type of information they receive from schools (Cuttance & Stokes, 2000).

Cuttance and Stokes (2000) further indicated that parents identified a number of concerns and improvements required in the reporting process:

- Parents believe there is a tendency, more common in primary schools, to avoid facing or telling hard truths. Parents understand how difficult it may be for teachers to convey "bad" news, but nevertheless they indicate that they want a "fair and honest" assessment, in plain language, of the progress of their children.
- There is a lack of objective standards that parents can use to determine their children's attainment and rate of progress. Many parents specifically asked for information that would enable them to compare their children's progress with that of other students or with agreed-upon state- or territorywide or national standards.
- Parents indicated they would like more interpretative and constructive reporting. Parents want something more substantial from reports than simple statements of achievement levels. They also want advice on what the report means in terms of the future learning goals for their child and how parents can support their children's learning.
- Most systems that report test results to parents do not require schools to incorporate these results in their reports to parents. Parents expressed a degree of confusion when they receive test

reports in one style and metric and school reports in another, unrelated style using a different metric.

- Parents want more comprehensible reports when they are based on outcomes reporting. Some education systems have adopted criterion-based outcomes-reporting approaches, but many parents are finding it difficult to understand the reports because of changes in assessment practices.
- Parents require more appropriate timing of reports. They indicated a clear preference for reports earlier each year when they are in a better position to support their children with learning improvement. Parents appreciated reports during Term 1, where these were provided, and find that an end-of-year report is too late for any constructive use.
- There is a mistrust of computer-generated reports in the parent community. Parents indicated that they find computer reports to be impersonal and limited. Parents want reports that are tailored to their individual children.
- Parent-teacher meetings need to be more useful to parents. Parents are dissatisfied with meetings that are poorly organized and lack focus and purpose. They consider meetings of 5–10 minutes to be too limited to be useful and believe they are organized mainly for ceremonial purposes. The timing of most meetings does not encourage an interactive discussion.
- The detection and prompt reporting of learning and behavioral problems is of major concern to parents. Many parents are concerned that they were advised as early as they could have been of their children's learning problems.
- Parents would like an enhanced role for their children in the reporting process. Parents believe that their children are an integral part of the reporting process and seek to involve them in parent-teacher meetings as well as in other aspects of assessment and reporting.

In light of the above information, you may want to provide a variety of opportunities to convey information to parents. Keep in mind that informed parents usually mean supportive parents. Uninformed parents may have a tendency to assume the worst, write negative scripts, interrogate their children, and be defensive. We suggest you try the following:

1. As previously mentioned, you should hold individual interviews with the parent(s) at the beginning of the year. This allows parents to give teachers firsthand information, which

will assist them in planning to meet the specific individual needs of each child.

2. Use a variety of progress reports that focus on the specific needs or concerns of the child instead of a general one that focuses on too many areas. For instance, if the parents of primary school children are not aware if homework has been given and need to know that it was turned in the next day, you might use the form shown in Figure 8.1.

**Figure 8.1**    Homework Tracking Form (Primary School)

**Elementary Grades**

Name:

Date:

_____**Monday**

| | | |
|---|---|---|
| Homework tonight | yes_____ | no____ |
| Homework handed in | yes_____ | no____ |

Comments:

_____**Tuesday**

| | | |
|---|---|---|
| Homework tonight | yes_____ | no____ |
| Homework handed in | yes_____ | no____ |

Comments:

_____**Wednesday**

| | | |
|---|---|---|
| Homework tonight | yes_____ | no____ |
| Homework handed in | yes_____ | no____ |

Comments:

_____**Thursday**

| | | |
|---|---|---|
| Homework tonight | yes_____ | no____ |
| Homework handed in | yes_____ | no____ |

Comments:

_____**Friday**

| | | |
|---|---|---|
| Homework tonight | yes_____ | no____ |
| Homework handed in | yes_____ | no____ |

Comments:

**Figure 8.2**    Homework Tracking Form (Secondary School)

Name:

Date: Monday _____

Subject

**Math**

| | | |
|---|---|---|
| Homework tonight | yes____ | no___ |
| Homework handed in | yes____ | no___ |

Comments:

**Social Studies**

| | | |
|---|---|---|
| Homework tonight | yes____ | no___ |
| Homework handed in | yes____ | no___ |

Comments:

**English**

| | | |
|---|---|---|
| Homework tonight | yes____ | no___ |
| Homework handed in | yes____ | no___ |

Comments:

**Science**

| | | |
|---|---|---|
| Homework tonight | yes____ | no___ |
| Homework handed in | yes____ | no___ |

Comments:

At the secondary level, you may want to use the form shown in Figure 8.2. This form would be completed for Monday, Tuesday, Wednesday, Thursday, and Friday school days.

This type of daily record will reinforce the child's accountability and assist the parents in working with the child at home. When you meet with the parents at the beginning of the year, explain that they should expect this form to come home every night.

Such progress reports are important sources of information on the child's learning at school. Do not be afraid to tailor such reports to specific behaviors if they are required to facilitate positive outcomes.

More detailed reports focusing on academic achievement, social abilities, cooperation, etc. should be done monthly with children with learning disabilities. However, have a policy that allows parents to request an interview with you at any time throughout the school year. Also, provide a system of communicating home on a regular basis to provide positive information, suggestions, solutions to issues you have noticed, or just to see if the parents have any concerns. Using this approach will facilitate closeness with the school and your educational plans, as discussed later in this section.

The specific type or types of grading systems for children with special needs should be chosen with sensitivity and a plan to improve self-esteem, not discourage or reinforce feelings of inadequacy.

# Step IX

# Developing Cooperative Educational Plans for Your Students

One of the most important approaches to the education of students with special needs is to develop a practical, worthwhile, and sound cooperative educational plan among you, your student, and your student's parent(s). These types of plans are used in many other professions to enhance the success rate in reaching the goals for an individual. For instance, in the medical field, this treatment plan usually involves several different personnel: the social worker, psychologist, and psychiatrist. In the educational field, such a plan usually only involves the teacher and the student, leaving out a very crucial factor in the child's chances for success in school, namely the parent. A cooperative educational plan that involves the school, the child, and the parent will have the greatest chance of helping the student succeed in school.

Cooperative educational plans for your students with special needs must be triangular plans. Coordination of services and techniques among the school, the child, and home will increase the chances of success for a child with special needs in school. Many times, only the school is involved with the child with the child being a passive recipient of services and the parents being onlookers. To increase the chances of success for the child, you need to coordinate the three sides of the cooperative educational plan.

One side of the triangle should be the school's responsibilities to help the child reach his or her potential. The school's responsibilities may include the following:

- Setting academic goals and objectives
- Determining and monitoring modifications
- Determining and modifying accommodations
- Developing the IEP
- Adapting the curriculum
- Determining the child's learning style
- Maintaining communication with the home
- Writing year-end reports
- Teaching the required curriculum
- Providing and monitoring related services
- Collaborating with the child's other teachers

You need to communicate and instruct the parents so that they are very clear as to their role in this process. The side of the educational plan that contains the responsibilities of the parents may include items such as the following:

- Make sure that homework is checked every night so that the child comes to school every day feeling a sense of accomplishment and avoiding a sense of embarrassment or failure.
- Contact you via mail, e-mail, or phone if the child has had difficulty with an assignment and needs to go over it again.
- Read to the child every night before bed if in elementary school and have the child read for 15 minutes every night if in secondary school. The reading should be of either the child's or parent's choice. Reading is reading, regardless of the content, and stress-free reading before bedtime is advisable. You do not want the child to go to sleep frustrated.
- Attend all conferences.
- Work with the child on homework in ways described later in this chapter.
- Help the child study for tests by following learning and studying guidelines set forth by you. Here you will have to instruct the parents carefully by giving specific directions about the appropriate study support procedures that will not frustrate the child.
- Ensure that the child begins studying for tests on the study start date indicated by you. This date should take into account the child's learning style.

- Return all progress reports on time with signatures indicating their awareness of the progress or concerns reported. Keep these in your files for accountability if a concern should arise.

The child makes up the third side of the triangle, and the child's involvement in this process is equally important. The student's responsibilities can be outlined in the form of a contract or letter. They should include the following:

- Finish homework every night or at least try as much as he understands.
- Allow the parent to check homework and suggest corrections. Note that you will have to work with parents on how to offer constructive suggestions versus criticism.
- Follow class rules.
- Begin studying for tests on the study start date you have set and communicated to the parents.
- Be able to approach the teacher when unable to do an assignment or not understanding a topic.

This plan should be written and given to all the parties involved if the age and developmental ability of the child allows for some understanding of responsibilities. This type of plan should work effectively with what we call high-incidence disabilities, namely those disabilities with the greatest number of students: learning disabilities, emotional disturbance, speech and language impairment, and mental retardation (higher-functioning). Other types of disabilities also could benefit from such a plan (e.g., ADHD).

# Step X

# End-of-School-Year Responsibilities

N ow that we are finally approaching the end of school, your
responsibilities are not yet over. This is a very important time
to make sure that each child's records are up-to-date and ready for the
coming year. This part of the year is crucial since it will define what
you have accomplished with parents and students. This is also when
certain legal requirements need to met, depending on the school district in which you are employed. So let's take these topics one at a
time so that you are prepared for each one. The topics covered in this
chapter include the following:

- Teacher reports for triennial evaluations
- Preparing for annual review meetings
- Declassification or decertification of students with learning
  disabilities
- Extended school year recommendations
- Writing end-of-school-year reports to parents

## Triennial Evaluation Reports

Every three years, beginning when the child was initially classified
by the IEP committee, a reevaluation takes place to assess the child's

current strengths and weaknesses, determine if the variables that determined the classification are still present to the level of significant impairment, and make recommendations based on the outcomes of the assessment. This assessment is very thorough, as defined in the law, and the results must be shared with the parents and the IEP committee. This is sometimes done at the annual review for that year.

As the child's classroom teacher, you will be asked by the assessment team, usually referred to as the "multidisciplinary team," to provide information on the child that will assist in these recommendations. According to Pierangelo (2004), this information, in the form of a report, should include the following:

- *The child's present academic levels in reading, math, spelling, and writing.* These may be available as a result of recent individual or group achievement tests, informal evaluations that you may have administered, observation (although try to be more objective), class tests, etc. Include grade levels of achievement, if possible, and where the child falls in comparison to others in the class. Also include samples of the child's work and describe the child's interest areas and areas of strength.
- *The child's present pattern of classroom behavior.* Write this up in behavioral terms (factual, observable, and descriptive notes of behavior that do not include analysis or judgment). Describe the child's present levels of social interaction and social skills.
- *Child's schedule.* Include a copy of the child's present schedule.
- *Physical limitations.* Note any physical limitations and their implication for the learning process.
- *Record of communications with parents.* Include an outline of parent conferences, phone conversations, and other meetings and the purpose and outcome of each. These notes should be kept on an ongoing basis.
- *Child's feedback.* Note any pertinent comments made by the child that may have an impact on the present situation.
- *Your opinion as to whether the child is benefiting from his or her present placement.*

## Annual Review Meetings

Beginning in March or April, depending on the school district, you will be asked to participate in annual review meetings. These meetings, which are required by law, are held by the IEP committee to review the child's progress over the past school year and make recommendations for the following school year. The parent or parents of the child usually attend this meeting, so being prepared is crucial. There are many things you will need to consider.

As with a regular IEP committee meeting, several people may attend this meeting. Who attends may vary from district to district and may include the following individuals:

- Director of special education services or assignee
- School psychologist
- Parent committee member
- Parent of the child
- Guidance counselor (secondary level)
- Assigned teacher. (At the secondary level, this may be the classroom teacher in a self-contained class, resource room teacher if this is the only service provided, or one of the child's special education teachers in a special education departmentalized program.)
- Classroom teacher (elementary level)
- Speech and language therapist (if the child's classification requires attendance)
- The child, if over a certain age (if the professionals feel that the child could benefit from the discussion or may be able to shed light on a concern or recommendation being considered)
- Any other individual deemed necessary

This meeting should be taken very seriously, since it will determine the child's educational direction and objectives for the coming year. As a result, you should be prepared and familiar with the following materials:

- Any pre- and poststandardized test scores indicating the child's academic progress for the year
- A copy of the child's report card clearly outlining grades and attendance for the year
- Suggested goals and objectives for the coming year
- An evaluation indicating whether or not the child benefited from the modifications allowed on his IEP and the reasons they may or may not have been beneficial
- If applicable, recommendations for additional test modifications
- If applicable, recommendations and rationale for additional related services

- If applicable, recommendations and rationale for reduction of related services
- Samples of the child's work over the course of the year
- A review of the child's overall social progress for the year

The above information should be sufficient to support a professional judgment of the child's progress and needs for the coming year (Pierangelo, 2004).

# Declassification Considerations and Procedures

A major component of special education reform effort is decertifying students no longer in need of special education services and, where necessary, providing support services and/or transitional services in general education. If declassification or decertification is determined to be necessary, you will be an active participant in this process.

During periodic reviews of the student's IEP (i.e., annual review, requested reviews, and triennial review), the IEP Committee (or the committee on special education) should determine if the student no longer requires special education services as the student's needs can be met in the general education program. This committee should also determine, for a student who no longer requires special education services, if the student requires temporary services to facilitate transition to general education (i.e., declassification support services). Students who will continue to require ongoing special education services for more than a year are not appropriate candidates for decertification at this time.

The IEP committee must make decisions regarding decertification on a case-by-case basis based on the needs of the student. The decertification process must comply with federal IDEA regulations and the board of education procedures for your district. This includes the active participation of the student's parents and the student, as appropriate, in the decision-making process. Under the reauthorized IDEA, parents also have the right to request that assessments be conducted.

Declassification support services are temporary services (not to exceed 12 months) designed to assist students who have been declassified from special education services and recommended for a general education program. Declassification support services provide temporary direct support to students and/or the receiving teacher to facilitate transition to the general education classroom and maintain appropriate student functioning. Declassification support services may include individual or group counseling, individual or group speech and language services, small-group instruction, modified curricula, or other strategies that have demonstrated success with students.

## Extended School Year (ESY) Services

One of the issues that you may need to consider is whether any of your students will need services over the summer to ensure that they do not lose what they have gained. These services are provided to maintain continuity of learning and make sure that the student does not fall behind for the coming school year. These services are called extended school year (ESY) services, and their appropriateness is determined by the IEP committee. Again, you will play a crucial role in this determination and should be aware of the requirements.

As part of the IEP process, a multidisciplinary team must determine if a child needs a program of special education and related services extending beyond the normal school year. For such a child, restricting services to a standard number of school days per year does not allow development of an education program that is truly individualized. A child may require ESY services to receive free and appropriate public education (FAPE).

Reasons why ESY services may be needed vary from child to child, but the end result is that some children suffer severe losses of social, behavioral, communication, academic, or self-sufficiency skills during interruptions in instruction. The determination of whether a child with a disability needs ESY services must be made on an individual basis following the IEP process. The critical question that each IEP team must ask regarding ESY services is whether the learning that occurred during the regular school year will be significantly jeopardized if ESY services are not provided.

Your role will include providing documentation to the committee. The primary criteria in determining a child's need for ESY services are the likelihood of significant regression of previously learned skills during a break in services and limited or delayed recoupment of these skills after services resume. The factors to be considered in making ESY placement decisions include, but are not limited to, the following:

*Category of disability.* Children with disabilities requiring consistent, highly structured programs may be predisposed to regression when their services are interrupted. These children may also have limited recoupment capacity.

*Severity of disability.* Although limited recoupment capacity can occur among children with moderate disabilities, it is more likely to be a learning characteristic of children with severe disabilities. Children with the most severe emotional disturbance, for example, are more likely to revert to lower-functioning levels or to exhibit inappropriate behaviors, such as extreme withdrawal or anxiety reactions, when their programs are interrupted. For many of these children, each successive interruption in programming and consequential regression also reduces the level of motivation and trust and may lead to an irreversible withdrawal from the learning process. Finally, children with severe disabilities are more likely to have difficulty attaining the goals of self-sufficiency and independence from caretakers and may need additional help and support to reach those goals.

*Parents' ability to provide an educational structure at home.* A parent or guardian may be unable to maintain a child's level of performance during a break in programming because of the complexity of the program, time constraints, lack of expertise, or other factors. This consideration is relevant to whether a child can be expected to regress. Also relevant is the child's stage of mastery of crucial skills or behavioral controls at the point of interruption in programming.

When appropriate, school districts should consider offering training to parents to help them maintain their child's level of performance during interruptions in programming. School districts may also consider offering support services in the home, either directly or in cooperation with other agencies, if such services will prevent the child's regression during breaks in programming. School districts are free to utilize the resources of other public or private agencies to meet the child's needs, as long as there is no cost or financial liability for the child's parents or guardians.

*Child's rate of progress.* Just as every child's rates of learning, regression, and recoupment are different from those of other children, an individual's rate of learning specific skills or behaviors may differ from the rate of attaining other skills. Certain skills or behaviors are particularly essential to meeting the goals of self-sufficiency. For example, basic self-help skills, such as toileting or eating, are essential for minimal independence; and stable relationships, impulse control, and appropriate peer interaction are necessary for community living. Therefore, if a child would suffer significant regression in a skill or behavior that is particularly crucial to reaching the goal of self-sufficiency and independence from caretakers, the child requires continuous education programming in that skill or behavior area.

Keep in mind that not all your students will require extended school year services. However, closely evaluate each child's needs and do not be afraid to suggest ESY services if you feel they might benefit the student. If you make this recommendation, you are offering the committee your professional judgment, and if you provide support for the above criteria, your presentation should be received as very professional.

## End-of-School-Year Reports

If your school district requires you to write end-of-school-year reports to parents, you will need to take several things into consideration. In general, you will want to use plain language, since most parents may not readily understand special education jargon. You may want to hold your own year-end meeting with all parents, even though you may have just seen them at an annual review meeting. At this meeting, you will want to discuss summer plans, extended school year services if applicable, the parent's role in maintaining learning over the summer, suggested materials and readings, and what to expect next year. At this meeting, you can go over your report orally, but make sure the parents have a professional-looking typed copy to take with them. When writing this report, keep the following in mind:

- The written report should provide information on what students have learned as a result of the school's teaching programs in each of the key learning areas.
- Information provided in the report should be consistent with syllabuses in each key learning area. Written reports may also provide additional information about student achievement in relation to school programs that extends beyond syllabus requirements or with respect to special needs.
- The written report should identify student strengths and areas that need further development or assistance.
- The written report should provide parents with information about the student's attendance at school.
- The written report should provide information about the student's social skills and development and commitment to learning.
- The written report may include information about student participation in other school programs (e.g., sports, leadership, clubs).

Try to keep the report to one page if possible. This can still be a lot of information for parents to grasp.

## Final Summary

This brings us to the end of a book that, we hope, will prepare you for what lies ahead in the teaching of students with disabilities. The purpose of the book is to cover as much as possible so that you can feel more comfortable with many of the issues you will face this school year. Although we are sure that you may encounter other aspects of teaching children with disabilities that we did not have room to cover, we have tried to provide you with a framework of issues that are normally experienced by teachers in your field. We hope this makes a difference for you in your job as a special education teacher. Good luck, stay calm, and be resourceful.

# Glossary

**Ability grouping**—The grouping of children based on their achievement in an area of study

**Accelerated learning**—An educational process that allows students to progress through the curriculum at an increased pace

**Achievement**—The level of a child's accomplishment on a test of knowledge or skill

**Adaptive behavior**—An individual's social competence and ability to cope with the demands of the environment

**Adaptive physical education**—A modified program of instruction implemented to meet the needs of special students

**Age norms**—Standards based on the average performance of individuals in different age groups

**Anecdotal record**—A procedure for recording and analyzing observations of a child's behavior; an objective, narrative description

**Baseline measure**—The level or frequency of behavior prior to the implementation of an instructional procedure that will later be evaluated

**Behavior modification**—Techniques used to change behavior by applying principals of reinforcement learning

**Categorical resource room**—An auxiliary pull-out program that offers supportive services to exceptional children with the same disability

**Consultant teacher**—A supportive service for disabled children in which services are provided by a specialist in the classroom

**Criterion-referenced tests**—Tests in which the child is evaluated on his own performance with reference to a set of criteria and not in comparison to others

**Declassification**—The process by which a disabled child is no longer considered in need of special education services. This requires a meeting of the eligibility committee and can be requested by the parent, school, or child if over the age of 18.

**Deficit**—A level of performance that is less than expected for a child

**Due process**—The legal steps and processes outlined in educational law that protect the rights of disabled children

**Dyscalculia**—A serious learning disability in which the child has an inability to calculate, apply, solve, or identify mathematical functions

**Dysgraphia**—A serious learning disability in which the child has an inability or loss of ability to write

**Dyslexia**—A serious learning disability in which a child's ability to read is greatly impaired

**Dysorthographia**—A serious learning disability that affects a child's ability to spell

**Inclusion**—Returning disabled children to their home school so that they may be educated with nonhandicapped children in the same classroom

**Individualized Educational Plan**—A written educational program that outlines a disabled child's current levels of performance, related services, educational goals, and modifications. This plan is developed by a team including the child's parent(s), teacher(s), and supportive staff.

**Intervention**—Preventive, remedial, compensatory, or survival services provided on behalf of a disabled individual

**Itinerant teacher**—A teacher hired by a school district to help in the education of a disabled child. The teacher is employed by an outside agency and may be responsible for several children in several districts.

**Least-restrictive environment**—Educating handicapped children with nonhandicapped children whenever realistic and possible; the least-restrictive setting in which the disabled child can function without difficulty

**Mainstreaming**—The practice of educating exceptional children in the regular classroom

**Mental age**—The level of intellectual functioning based on the average for children of the same chronological age. When dealing with severely disabled children, the mental age may be more reflective of levels of ability than the chronological age.

**Noncategorical resource room**—A resource room in regular school that provides services to children with all types of classified disabilities who can be maintained in a regular classroom.

**Norm-referenced tests**—Tests used to compare a child's performance to the performance of others on the same measure

**Related services**—Services provided to disabled children to assist with their ability to learn and function in the least-restrictive environment, including in-school counseling, speech and language services, and so on

# References

British Columbia Ministry of Education, Special Education Services. (2006). Retrieved August 7, 2007, from www.bced.gov.bc.ca/specialed/

Cuttance, P., & Stokes, S. (2000). *Reporting on student and school achievement.* Canberra, Australia: Commonwealth Department of Education, Training and Youth Affairs.

Friend, M., & Bursuck, W. D. (2005). *Including students with special needs: A practical guide for classroom teachers* (4th ed.). Boston: Allyn & Bacon.

Houghton Mifflin Education Place. (2006). *Setting up your classroom.* Retrieved August 7, 2007, from www.eduplace.com/rdg/res/classroom.html

Individuals with Disabilities Education Act (IDEA), 34 C.F.R. § 300.24(a) (2004).

Johnson Smith, K. (n.d.). *Twelve rules for arranging your classroom.* Retrieved April 3, 2007, from the University of North Carolina Chapel Hill, School of Education, Learn NC, Web site: www.learnnc.org/lp/pages/first year-12rules

Pierangelo, R. (2004). *The special educator's survival guide.* San Francisco: Jossey Bass.

Salend, S. (2001). *Creating inclusive classrooms: Effective and reflective practices* (4th ed.). Upper Saddle River, NJ: Merrill Prentice Hall.

Villa, R., Thousand, J., & Chapple, J. (1996). Preparing teachers to support inclusion: Preservice and inservice programs. Inclusive schools: The continuing debate [Special issue]. *Theory into Practice, 35*(1), 42–50.

Wunder, M., & Lindsey, C. (2006). The ins, outs of co-teaching [Electronic version]. *Missouri Innovations in Education, 23*(4). Retrieved August 7, 2007, from http://radnortsd.schoolwires.com/

# Index

Age equivalent, 3
Alternate teaching, 28
Annual review meetings, 90–92

Child-oriented model, 13
Communication, 19–35
  with aide, 25
  with assistant teacher, 25
  with inclusion team teacher, 27
  with parents (elementary), 19
  with parents (secondary), 24
  with related-service providers, 29
  with the mainstreaming team, 32
  with your student's regular
    education teacher, 30
Complementary instruction, 27
Cooperative educational plans, 85–87
Curriculum adaptations
  examples, 44
  ways to adapt, 46
  adapting response mode, 51

Declassification considerations, 92

Emotional disturbance, 59–60
End-of-school-year reports, 95–96
Evaluating existing materials, 16–18
Extended school year services
  (ESY), 93–95

Factors affecting curriculum
  academic factors, 36–37
  environmental factors, 37–38
  intellectual factors, 38
  language factors, 38–39
  medical factors, 39–40
  perceptual factors, 40
  psychological factors, 40–41
  social factors, 42

Gathering information
  group achievement scores, 2
  history of educational enrollment, 2
  medical background, 2
  past teacher comments, 10
  primary record folder in main
    office, 2
  prior comments from
    past teachers, 2
  report card history, 2
Grade equivalent, 3
Grading options, 77

Individualized Education
  Programs (IEP)
  accommodations, 8
  annual goals, 6
  assistive technology, 9
  classification, 8
  health alerts, 8
  measuring progress, 7
  modifications, 8
  participation with nondisabled
    students, 6
  present levels of educational
    performance, 6
  related services, 8
  special education and related
    services, 6
  transition goals and
    services, 7
Instructional interventions
  active noncompliance, 61–63
  attendance problems, 63–64
  classroom disruption, 67–68
  difficulty with transitions, 65–66
  disrespect to teachers, 66–67
  failure to accept responsibility, 69
  interpersonal relationships, 70

not respecting personal
     space, 73–74
out-of-control behaviors, 71–73
passive resistance, 71
verbal aggression, 74–75
verbal outbursts, 75–76

Learning disabilities, 53–56
Local percentile, 3

Mean, 3
Mental retardation, 56–58

National percentile, 3

Parallel teaching, 28
Parent conferences, 19

Range, 4
Raw score, 4
Reporting progress to parents, 79

Scaled Score, 4
Standard deviation, 5
Standard score, 5
Stanine, 5
Station oriented model, 11
Station teaching, 28

T score, 6
Teacher oriented model, 13
Team teaching, 29
Triennial evaluation reports, 89–90

z score, 6